Reviews

"When I first joined Peachbowl Dawnbreakers Toastmasters in Yuba City, California, just on the other side of the river from Linda, I met Bob Gauper at a club meeting on Zoom. He seemed relatively quiet for a Toastmaster and yet impressed me almost immediately as a very knowledgeable and thoughtful individual. Frequently, Bob would make a comment that I always found instructive, often humorous, and always with a little bit of an unexpected twist.

Once I asked my fellow Toastmasters if any of them would consider volunteering to be speech judges for the upcoming Yuba City Rotary Speech Contest. Bob immediately volunteered and later called me and told me his wife Maree was also a Toastmaster in a different club and she would enjoy being part of the judging team.

That was how I met both Bob and his wife in person after only knowing Bob from our Toastmaster meetings on Zoom. Right away I was really impressed with Maree. She is a class act lady and it was evident to me that Bob and Maree had a really solid marriage. Little did I realize how truly unique their relationship was until reading *Leaving Linda*.

One day out of the blue after I had left Toastmasters due to my overcommitment to Rotary programs, Bob called and asked if I would mind being a "Beta Reader" for his new book, *Leaving Linda*. I couldn't help but think, "I wonder if Bob had been previously married, and his wife was named Linda?" He explained that *Leaving Linda* was about his childhood in Linda, and how he decided to leave Linda to experience the world.

I immediately responded that I would be quite honored to read *Leaving Linda* and write a review. There was no hesitation on my part to this request because I just had a feeling that anything Bob wrote would be quite interesting as well as entertaining to read. Primarily because his Toastmaster speeches were often unique and engaging. There was no way Bob Gauper would write a boring book about his life and boy was I right on that assumption.

After downloading *Leaving Linda* to my Kindle, I knew after the first page that it was going to be an adventure. I was completely hooked by just that first page and that was only the beginning.

Throughout the book, he takes what I call a normal situation and throws something "off the wall" into the story. These happenings had to be true, no one could possibly invent such unique adventures without having experienced them.

I already had a strong belief that Bob and Maree have a positive marriage based upon my observation of how they interact with each other as well as comments Bob has personally made. I was completely blown away with how they met, were married, and even spent the first years of their marriage as described in *Leaving Linda*.

One thing I can absolutely guarantee, if you read *Leaving Linda*, you are going to have so many special memories of Bob's life that are going to just stick in your mind. Bob's wanderlust in his youth and life adventures were quite spontaneous and I could not help but think "WOW" to his description of his innermost thoughts during these experiences.

I do a lot of reading. Bob's book is special in that you will feel like you are present with Bob experiencing his life. It is a great book and I highly recommend it."

— **Bill Highland**, retired, Yuba City HS Administrator, Rotary Club President

"Leaving Linda is the story of a man who was willing to say 'YES!' to life's adventures. It starts in a small town and ends half a world away."

—**"Farmer Jim" Muck**, University of California, Davis

"My adventures with 'Bullet Bob': Parasailing pioneers at Lake Tahoe, scary hitch-hiking rides down Tioga pass, Yosemite, Big Fork, Minnesota, the St. Louis Fish House, etc. Proud to be a small part of a good friend's book."

— **Larry French**, Peoria, Illinois

"A well written memoir. I enjoyed how the story moved from an ordinary childhood in a small town in Northern California to an anything but ordinary journey through life."

— **Joe Waggershauser**

Leaving Linda
A Moonie from the Boonies

Robert J. Gauper

Contents

Copyright

This book is a work of creative non-fiction. Some of the places, people, animals, and scenes may have been changed to protect the innocent, guilty, or because this nearly seventy-year-old forgets stuff.

"Moonie" is an often-derogatory word referring to the members of the Unification church, founded in Korea in 1954 by Sun Myung Moon. Many members prefer to identify themselves as "Unificationists", which unfortunately does not rhyme with boonies.

Visit LeavingLinda.com for additional stories and information.

Dedication

To kind and sincere people. God knows who you are.

Foreword

Hi, I'm a life story junkie. I look for people whose words are compelling and have the ring of truth. That's why I'm thrilled to recommend *Leaving Linda* by Bob Gauper for its combination of interesting storytelling and authenticity.

From the time of his parents' coming of age in semirural canoe country Minnesota, in the chilly north woods a few miles south of Canada, his father and mother migrated to where the work was for surveying and public works jobs that took them to Idaho, Washington State and into northern California to a little bitty town called Linda.

Linda has a feature in common with every other small town in America. It's relatively safe and, temporary insanities aside, predictable. It seems to an outsider to be idyllic, Norman Rockwellian. But when you're growing up in this mom and dad America, you can't wait to graduate high school and put your hometown squarely in the rearview mirror.

Unless we were really sheltered growing up, most of us did some dumb stuff and took a few chances that could have gotten us killed. Jumping off a high cliff into unknown water comes to mind. But those are the extremes, and most of the time we recall our adventures with fondness – hitchhiking, putting up with shop-lifting con artist roommates; getting chased by a drunk with a broken beer bottle for selling flowers in a bar, to raise money for his church. You know, the usual.

Bob's disillusionment with a rootless life working in Las Vegas casinos exposed an emptiness that led to an epic search for deeper meaning. Epic searches for truth eventually bring you to that fork in the road which, in one direction, leads to a normal life, "picket fence and nine to five" as Bob writes, and maybe love. Or down the other road to God knows where. Literally.

There's a great deal of thoughtfulness in Bob's story. That comes partly with age and introspection, and also with having a fierce sense of purpose and the determination to work through life's distractions, sidetracks and bad choices (of which they are legion and familiar to all) to end up being married to the love of his life and to have made and raised a family with Maree (a Kiwi) and their children.

The writing in this book is descriptive and highly relatable. There were times I saw myself painted into the tapestries he weaves. I know that's happening when I find myself reading the dialogue aloud. And some parts are damned funny.

A well-rendered warts-and-all memoir is hard to come by. But it's here in these pages, and that's why you should read it. This is a fine tale, factual and enhanced with photos and illustrations by Maree. Welcome to an honest account of a man's life, told in a way that sets a high bar for the telling of one's own story.

Larry Moffitt

Author of *Searching for San Viejo: Notes to My Younger Self,* Bowie, Maryland

October 10, 2022

Introduction

In 1978, at the age of twenty-four, I left my hometown of Linda, California, on a quest which led this restless country boy to an unexpected spiritual path.

Instead of a hermit on a sailboat, I became a pioneer for a new and idealistic religious movement as well as a husband and father.

This is my story.

Linda Map

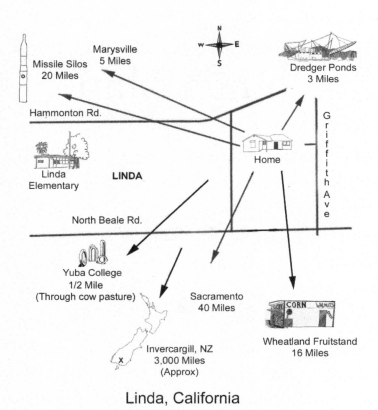

Linda, California

Chapter One

Axe Man

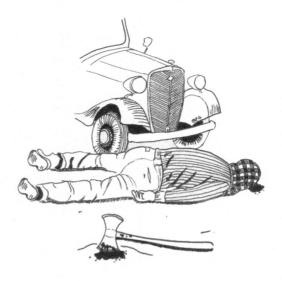

It's January 1947. Blood oozes from the young man's head, slowly staining the freshly fallen snow, then stops. A curious young deer stands nearby as the soothing hum of the truck engine, *Chevy's Cast Iron Wonder,* breaks the winter silence. Warm air from the truck's exhaust billows upward into the Minnesota sky. Water drips from the tailpipe onto the ground and freezes. Like a primitive timepiece, each drip counts the seconds as the frozen mound grows taller.

Faint puffs of fog from the man's nostrils signal that he's breathing. The deer scurries off as the man begins to move and crawl toward his bloodied axe. He uses the axe to steady himself as he stands up and staggers toward the truck.

Thank God the truck's still running. I couldn't have been passed out too long. Otherwise it would have run out of gas.

He opens the door, climbs inside then looks into the mirror and sees a gash on his forehead and in his lumberjack cap. He reaches for the gearshift and shifts into reverse to turn around. He stops and shifts into first. Suddenly blood squirts from his wound and onto the windshield. He stops the bleeding with his right hand.

The cold air must have slowed down the bleeding. It's too hot in here.

He rolls down the window and drives forward while still pressing the wound then moves his hand to shift into second. Blood sprays the windshield. Third gear. More blood.

I gotta get outta here. If not, I'm a goner. Shit. I'm almost out of gas. Hope I can make it. I can barely see out the window.

He steadies the steering wheel with his right elbow then wipes the windshield with his left hand.

Dammit, that made it worse. I can't see! He stops pressing the wound then thrusts his head out the window to see the road ahead. The frigid air soon stops the bleeding. *There's a cabin about a mile up. I'll stop there. God, I hope someone's home.*

As he approaches the cabin, he sees smoke coming from the chimney.

Thank God.

He stops the truck, walks up to the cabin, and knocks on the door. A gray-haired woman opens it.

"I need some help. I --" Before he can explain she screams loudly, apparently horrified by the sight of a bloodied stranger on her doorstep.

Bam! The door's slammed shut.

Dammit!

He totters back to the truck.

Hope I can make it to the Olsons' place. It's a couple more miles. They'll help. Gotta stay conscious. Gotta stay awake.

The truck swerves as it heads down the snow-covered dirt road.

Almost there. Almost there.

He pulls into the Olsons' driveway and sees Klaus about a hundred yards away chopping wood near the barn.

Honk! Honk! The truck stops. It's out of gas. He leans onto the horn button and passes out.

∞

"Nice to see you're finally awake. You've lost a lot of blood. You're lucky to be alive John. What the heck happened?"

"Well, Doc, I had Ray Sorenson make a road with his dozer to a grove of pine I'll be cutting. He'd missed a stump and I tried to chop it up. Damn thing musta bin froze solid. My double-edge axe bounced back and hit me."

"If it wasn't for your cap, you probably would have died."

The doctor hands him his wool plaid lumberjack hat.

"See that gash in the bill? Looks like it softened the blow to your head. You oughta contact the manufacturer and tell them their cap saved your life.

"I'd like you to spend the night in the hospital. You should be able to go home tomorrow. Yep, you're one lucky man. Someone must be looking out for you."

As the doctor leaves the room, John touches the gash in his cap.

Yep, I'm one lucky guy. The cap. Waking up before the truck ran out of gas. Klaus. The cold weather.

He could never forget the day his gunnery crew was killed aboard the USS New Mexico by a kamikaze pilot. John was safe below deck in sick bay after bumbling sailors dropped a torpedo on his foot. Those Squids saved his life.

John looks out the hospital window. It's snowing again. He clutches the cap to his chest, like a child snuggling a teddy bear, then falls asleep.

Chapter Two

Down by the Riverside

John gently rubbed the scar on his forehead, then took the small canoe that was leaning against the barn and placed it on the ground. Of his three different canoes, he preferred the smallest one. It was faster and more maneuverable. The others were for cargo, like the wild rice Johnny and his brothers used to harvest.

He wouldn't be harvesting much wild rice anymore. Gone were the days when he, and his brothers Chet and Morrie, would spend weeks at a time canoeing the lakes and rivers of Northern Minnesota, searching for, and harvesting that wild grain prized for its dark color and nut-like flavor.

Chet even had an article about their adventures published in a major newspaper.

There wasn't much money in wild rice now that the government was controlling the harvest and requiring people to get permits.

He thought about selling the large canoes. Maybe some tourist from the Twin Cities would buy them once summer was here.

His dog Skippy jumped into the canoe as Johnny dragged it to the edge of the lake. Just as he was about to launch, his mother came out of the farmhouse.

"Johnny, here's some things I need from the store. Have them charge it to my account."

"Sure Mom. Should be back before dark."

He hoped he wouldn't forget that errand. He had a lot on his mind.

He watched his mother as she walked away and wondered how she was doing. Her husband, Alfred, Johnny's dad, didn't have much longer to live. Alfred had purchased the small farm for his retirement as a street-car-operator in Duluth. A year after his retirement, he was diagnosed with Multiple Sclerosis, and wasn't expected to live much longer. Johnny moved to the farm after he had purchased it from his parents. He was a bit surprised that the Farmers Home Administration approved the farm loan. He didn't know much about farming. But he got the loan. He'd just have to make a go of it.

His Dad's upcoming death troubled Johnny. He'd seen death on the battleship U.S.S. New Mexico, men right in front of him killed by Japanese gunfire. He saw a man whose head was blown off, running around the deck like the chickens Johnny used to butcher. It was creepy enough to watch chickens run around the barnyard with their heads chopped off. But a fellow human being… it was nearly too much to handle. He tried hard to keep that image out of his mind.

But his dad's approaching death was different. He was losing his battle with MS and fading away ounce by ounce. He looked to weigh only about eighty pounds now. Johnny always wondered when he was gone from the farm, if he'd come back to find his father dead. *Please don't let it happen today*, he prayed as he pulled the canoe to the shoreline.

He launched the canoe for what would probably be his last trip of the season. Ice was starting to form on the lake. Soon it would be frozen. Winter would be here, and people from town would be out on the lake setting up their shacks for ice fishing.

That was how he first met Maxine, his girl. She had come to the lake with her parents to do some ice fishing. Johnny had never seen her before that since she had caught tuberculosis while studying nursing and had been confined to a sanitarium in Minneapolis. When she occasionally came home for visits, he would now try to see her whenever possible.

Maxine was out of the sanitarium now; her health was improving, and she had a part-time job at Bigfork's movie theater. That's where she would be today. He'd catch her between the mid-day matinee and the evening showing.

They made a handsome couple. Him the six foot two, dark haired Marine veteran who kept in shape canoeing and working hard on the farm. Her, with her petite five-foot-five figure, gray eyes, and mischievous smile.

Johnny pushed off, hopped into the canoe, sat, and started to paddle off. The thin ice cracked and parted as the canoe floated forward. It made him think of when he was a merchant marine on a ship delivering much-needed supplies to the Russian port of Archangel in the White Sea, the winter of 1943.

The Russians had carved a path through the frozen port with their icebreakers, so Johnny's ship could have its cargo unloaded. Most of that job was done by prisoners of the Red Army. These walking dead, to ease their hunger, would somehow break into the cans of food they were unloading. Johnny often wondered how they managed without knives or can-openers. Desperate men, desperate for food.

Johnny spent nearly four months stuck in that port. It was too dangerous to leave because the Germans were attacking ships in the North Sea. While they waited for an armed escort to protect them as they sailed towards England, the ship, now loaded with lumber, sat ice-bound and motionless in the frozen sea.

One day Johnny threw a large garbage can of food scraps and frozen potatoes out onto the ice surrounding the ship. Quickly a large crowd gathered to fight over the garbage.

But that was a different time. The war was over, and Johnny was almost thirty years old. He'd had enough excitement in his life. Now was a time to be grateful to be an American and to live in a country of such freedom and such bounty.

It was time to settle down.

As he paddled away, Johnny glanced at the farmhouse and then the lake. A loon was making its usual strange noises, earning its reputation, crazy as a loon.

The trip into Bigfork wouldn't take too long, it was only about two miles. He paddled around the peninsula they called Piney Point. It was covered with virgin pines that were never cut down. This was surprising, since the trees stood so near to the lake. It would have taken little effort to harvest them and float them down the Rice River to the sawmill in Bigfork. Locals said the pines remained because the peninsula was once a burial ground for Chippewa Indians. Johnny would often walk through those woods looking for Indian artifacts, but without much luck.

He paddled past the point and into the slow-flowing river that would take him into Bigfork. As he entered the river, he saw a small otter dive underwater. Skippy barked loudly and wagged her tail profusely.

"Settle down girl. We're not goin' after that one," Johnny said softly as he paddled near where the otter disappeared.

When he used to set traps, Skippy would run up to a trap and bark until Johnny would either pick up the animal, or if it was empty, re-bait and set it. Without her help, the traps would be harder to find. Skippy made the work more efficient and was a good companion.

These days Johnny didn't have the heart to trap. Not since he'd found a fox's leg stuck in a trap, where a desperate creature had chewed off its own limb to save itself. The bloody trail of a three-legged animal had made him sick that day. He unchained the trap from the tree and went on to pick up the others. His trapping days were over. Besides, the fur looked fine on the otter.

Once he got into Bigfork, Johnny pulled the canoe to shore under the pedestrian bridge that linked downtown with the high school, then secured the canoe with a rope to a small bush.

"I'll be right back, Skippy. Sit! Stay!"

Skippy whimpered sadly, but she'd stay near the canoe. She was well-trained and obedient.

Johnny looked at his watch. It was half an hour until the movie ended. There was time to get what his mother needed at the grocery store.

He took the list out of his shirt pocket, knowing there wasn't much on it. They were well stocked for the winter.

His mother was a great cook, having worked at a camp for lumberjacks before marrying. She then went on to cook for her husband and seven kids. It was no exaggeration when Johnny told people his mother spent half her life in front of a stove. And he learned a lot from her.

The farm was well prepared for the long winter. His mother had canned wild blueberries, chokecherries, tomatoes, cucumbers, wild strawberries, and rhubarb. The root-cellar was filled with potatoes, squash, and wild rice. Eggs would come from the chickens, milk and butter from the cows, fresh fish from the lake, and Johnny and his brothers would kill some deer to supply meat.

Hunting season would start soon, although most locals didn't pay attention to any actual season. If you used the game to feed your family, the game warden usually left you alone.

Johnny looked at the shopping list: sugar, baking powder, salt, and some blackberry brandy.

At the Piggly Wiggly he picked up the supplies, plus some bones for Skippy.

"I heard about your mishap with that axe. Looks like that scar's healing up nicely," the store owner said as Johnny approached the cash register.

"Thankfully, it is."

"Say hello to your mom and dad for me. I miss seein' 'em."

"I'll do that."

Johnny walked to the theater, which wasn't far. Bigfork only had five-hundred residents.

Maxine was stocking the snack bar when he walked in.

"You almost done?"

"Yeah, sure. I have to be back in a couple of hours. What's up?"

"Wanna go to the river? Skippy's down by the canoe. I bought her some bones."

"Sounds good. Let's go."

As they walked down to the canoe Skippy started barking and wagging her tail, but still didn't move from her position. They sat down on the riverbank. He opened the bag of groceries, pulled out the bones and threw them near Skippy.

"Get 'em, girl!" The small dog bolted toward her treats.

Johnny and Maxine snuggled tightly to warm themselves, as they sat on the riverbank watching Skippy enjoy her cow bones. The water gently flowed past, moving the reeds and making the special soothing, hypnotic sound that rivers make. They sat in near silence as Johnny picked up some pebbles and threw them in the river. *Plop. Plop.* The splashes echoed under the bridge.

"You're quieter today than usual," Maxine whispered as she snuggled closer.

"Yeah, I've been thinkin' a lot about something important. Max, will you marry me?"

Johnny and Maxine (aka Dad and Mom) get Married

Chapter Three
Westward Bound

The rain came. A thunderous rain. A deluge. Rain to fill Rice Lake and the nearby river. Rain for the forest. Rain to bring life...and despair.

Johnny had worked all night planting the last rows of seed potatoes when it started. It hadn't stopped for days. Rain, rain, rain. The first planting froze and now the second planting was rotting away, along with his dreams of becoming a successful farmer.

"I knew you wouldn't make it as a farmer. You don't know what you're doing, and you don't have enough acreage. You should get a job at the mine."

That was what Maxine's mother would most likely say if he asked her and Slim for money for more seed potatoes.

Blah, blah, blah. God, that woman can jabber. No wonder they call her the Battle-Axe of Bigfork.

No wonder Max and her dad, Slim, drank so much. Johnny needed to get her out of there. Maybe he would take that offer to sell some acreage. His best friend Jack had been bugging him to join him in California. Maybe he would just do that.

While holding a lipstick-stained cigarette, Max adjusted the rearview mirror on the Plymouth her parents had given them for a wedding present and looked at them as she and Johnny drove away.

"They look sad. Probably wish they would have offered us money for more seed potatoes. Maybe we'd have been able to stay."

"Maybe yes, maybe no. So many maybes. We're headed west now, no lookin' back. Besides, this'll be better for your health. How you feelin' anyway? You're lookin' good."

"I'm feeling fine. Thanks for the compliment. You're not looking too bad yourself, husband. Better keep your eyes on the road though. Don't want us hitting a deer as we're leaving town. How far are we going 'til we stop for the night?"

"Like to make it to Jamestown. There's a motel we used to stay at when me an' Jack and my brother Morrie were balin' hay in the Dakotas. Be a lot different stayin' with you, 'stead of those loud, stinky workmates."

He put his hand on top of Max's leg and squeezed softly.

"You can go further if you'd like."

He moved his hand slowly up her leg.

"Um, I was thinking Dickerson."

After spending the night in Jamestown, they continued west. Near Boise, Idaho, Johnny stopped for gas and an oil change, and asked the station owner about a good place for lunch.

"There's a diner 'bout two miles up the road. Here's my car keys. You can borrow my car. I'll have the oil changed before you get back."

"You'll let me borrow your car? You don't even know me."

"No, I don't. But I do have your Plymouth and it's a lot newer and nicer than mine."

"Didn't think about that. Won't be too long. We'll get a bite to eat and be right back."

During lunch, Johnny asked Maxine if she'd like to stay in Boise. The people were friendly, and it seemed like a nice place to live. After picking up the car they located a motel and ironically, Johnny soon found a job, helping a farmer plant potatoes. He liked working for the farmer until he noticed his first paycheck was less than expected.

"Why's my paycheck so low?"

"Oh, ten percent goes to the church."

"What church?"

"LDS."

"What church is that?"

"The Mormons."

"*What?* You donated ten percent of my money to the Mormons? If I'm gonna give any money to a church, it'll be the Lutherans. I want the rest of my money."

"Sorry, I thought you were LDS like everyone else around here. I'll add ten percent to next week's paycheck."

Johnny continued working for the farmer until he was offered a job with the US Bureau of Reclamation at the Anderson Ranch Dam near Mountain Home, about an hour's drive from Boise, and moved there. While working at the dam, he learned surveying. He also learned he was going to be a father. On April 13th, 1954, Maxine gave birth to a bright and handsome red-haired boy. They named him Robert John, but mostly called him Bobby.

Johnny enjoyed his work. He loved being outside perfecting his skills as a surveyor. The math was hard, but Maxine helped him with that. He was worried about her though. So far from family and friends and a baby to take care of. They still weren't sure if they wanted to settle in the area and Jack was still bugging them to move to California. Moving or staying was always on his mind. He wasn't sure what to do. Until one day, when he was called into the office.

"I've got good and bad news, John," the construction supervisor said. "Most of our work is done here. It looks like we'll be looking for work elsewhere soon."

"What's the good news?"

"Well, I'll be heading up a crew building irrigation canals in Washington. I'd like you to join me."

"Where in Washington?"

"Mesa. It's a little hole-in-the-wall town in the desert. We'll be provided housing. Nothing much. Some kind of prefabricated living quarters."

And that was how my parents' Westward journey from Minnesota continued even further Westward, and even closer to Linda, California.

Chapter Four

What If?

"So, you guys happy with the move?" Johnny's supervisor asked.

"Yeah. Never lived in the desert before. Or in a tin shed. But it's all right. Most important, Max is happy. She likes workin' in the office part time and loves her bridge games with your wife."

"Gladys says Maxine is pretty smart."

"She sure is. She was high school valedictorian. Although there were only five people in the graduatin' class and her mother was the school principal, but still."

"Too bad we'll only be here a few more months. Any future plans?"

"Bin applyin' for jobs in California."

"Any prospects?"

"Well, yeah. Bin offered a job by the state. Department of Public Works. Settin' grade for Interstate 80 through the Sierra Nevada mountains and livin' in Truckee. I start in two months."

"Truckee? I've been skiing near there. Close to the Nevada border, west of Reno. Gets tons of snow and really cold in the winter. But you're from Minnesota, you can handle it. You ski?"

"A little. Used to ski jump."

"Ski jump? You got more balls than me. I hear the Winter Olympics is going to be at Squaw Valley. Maybe you could be on the ski jump team."

"Naw. Got a family to consider now. Another baby on the way. My ski jumpin' days are over."

John loved the small mountain town of Truckee. He got a super deal on a cute rental cabin within walking distance of downtown. A neighbor taught him fly fishing in the abundant nearby streams. Work was stressful, though. The extra money as Crew Chief was nice but he hated the responsibility. One of his biggest problems was nearby Reno.

"Good thing we get paid monthly," John confided to his supervisor one Monday morning. "Bet half the crew won't show up today. Or I'll have to send 'em home cuz they're too hung over."

"I know what you mean. Reno's temptations are hard to resist. How come you never go there?"

"Waste o' money. I like fishin' and spendin' time with the family. Might go to a local bar now and then."

The supervisor nodded thoughtfully, then asked, "So, how's Maxine's pregnancy going?"

"It's okay. She's bored though. Not much for her to do around here."

"Which leads me to suggest you consider moving elsewhere, John. Your wife needs a proper hospital to have her baby in and more people around. You can transfer to Sacramento if you'd like."

In about a month, Johnny got a job with the Sacramento Department of Public Works (now CalTrans) and he and Maxine moved to Marysville where his old friend Jack lived.

"So, if it wasn't for Greg, I might have grown up in Truckee? I think I might have really liked it," I told my dad years later.

"Perhaps. There was lots of work around. Looks like your brother was causin' you trouble even before he was born."

What if?

What if my parents would have stayed in Minnesota? Or Idaho? Or the picturesque town of Truckee? What would my life have been like?

However, I didn't grow up in those places. I grew up in Linda. Linda, California.

Chapter Five

Linda

Linda, California.

If you searched for it on the internet in 2018 you wouldn't have found much, mostly references to such places as Yorba Linda, Loma Linda, Terra Linda, and Rio Linda. That is, unless you typed a minus sign in front of those names to eliminate them from the Google search. But still not much would have come up besides images of flooding, the once thriving and now nearly vacant Peach Tree Mall, homes for sale on the ominously named Edgewater subdivision, and mentions of my blog, *Leaving Linda*.

Linda means beautiful in Spanish. It's also the name of a pioneer steamer that traveled up the Yuba River and a company that tried to set up a town in 1879. That town, consisting of a house, store, and two or three small buildings, was short-lived and after a couple of years it was deserted. The dream of a town called Linda was abandoned.

In 2022, even though the area has nearly 20,000 residents, Linda still isn't an official town. It's considered a Census Designated Place (CDP) by the U.S. Census Bureau. Some of the CDPs in the United States such as Bethesda, Maryland, and Montecito, California, are very exclusive. Linda is not one of them. In 2011, the per capita income was below $15,000.

I grew up in that CDP about 45 miles north of Sacramento, in deeply conservative Yuba County. In 1957 when I was three years old, my parents rented an apartment near my dad's friend Jack in Marysville. Soon after my younger brother was born, they wanted a bigger place and moved across the river, to 6088 Dunning Avenue, a rental property walking distance from Linda Elementary, where I would soon attend kindergarten.

When Dad told his workmates in Marysville that he'd moved to Linda, many protested. "You don't want to live there! That's where all the Okies and Arkies are." (Economic refugees from Oklahoma and Arkansas moved to the Linda area during the Great Depression to escape the Dust Bowl and to work in the numerous orchards nearby.)

Dad didn't listen to those naysayers, and a couple of years later with the help of the in-laws, bought a house on a three-acre parcel, at the end of a dirt road off Griffith Ave.

Slim and Jenny, my mother's parents from Northern Minnesota, had grand plans of escaping their frigid winters by towing a travel-trailer to my parents' property and living there during their coldest months. That plan barely lasted one season.

My grandparents, like many others, thought California was a place of abundant sunshine, movie stars, and ocean views. In my early twenties when I first met one of my Midwestern cousins on a trip to Minnesota, he asked me how I liked surfing.

"Huh? Man, the ocean's at least two hours away from where I live. I've never gone surfing."

Besides, we never owned a car that could make it that far. I'd seen the ocean only a couple of times by then, and that was on school trips.

Compared to Northern Minnesota, winters in Linda are rather mild. But it can and does rain a lot. Dense fog often sets in for weeks at a time, and the California sun can seem to be only a memory. For a variety of reasons, including unexpected severe weather and perhaps some family problems, Slim and Jenny from Bigfork would be towing their travel-trailer to Mesa, Arizona for future winters.

∞

The northern end of Griffith Avenue stops at Hammonton-Smartsville Road. That's where I would turn left toward Marysville. Often, I would tell myself:

"One of these days, I'm not going to turn left. I'm going to turn right and head to highway 20, turn east and keep driving. One of these days, I'm going to leave Linda."

Chapter Six

Linda Elementary

Johnnie's Market in 2022 - Steel posts installed after my mother
plowed into the building with our pickup

My elementary school was approximately a ten-minute walk from where we used to live on Dunning Avenue. It was past a few houses and a field filled with wildflowers, which drew bees, butterflies, and ladybugs. It was the ladybugs that got me and my friend Becky in trouble.

One day, while walking to school through the field, to our kindergarten class, we decided to study ladybugs along the way.

"Look, look!" Becky giggled when she spotted a ladybug crawling near a lavender-colored flower and gently picked it up.

"Hold out your arm," she whispered and gently placed the insect on my freckled forearm.

"Don't move. I'm going to find more."

I watched the lone orange bug crawl around my arm. It must have been terribly confused. I softly sang, "Ladybug, ladybug, fly away home. Your house…" It flew away. I gulped. Becky came back with another one.

"Where's the ladybug?"

"It flew away."

"Why?"

"I don't know. Maybe it's hungry. Or scared." I kept my singing a secret.

She opened her hand to show me her new prisoner, which briefly crawled around her hand then flew away too. I was relieved. A black and white butterfly fluttered by.

"Let's follow it," Becky murmured.

We shadowed the insect as it flew from flower to flower. We were having so much fun. Abruptly, our enjoyment was over.

"Get to class right now! You're late again. I'm going to talk to your parents!" Mrs. Clark, our teacher, cried out as she ran toward us. She grabbed our arms and hurried her wayward students to the classroom. After that, our nature expeditions were over. A parent would always walk us to school. They didn't have time for ladybugs.

In third grade I was a Cub Scout. I remember standing at the school flagpole while my buddy Mickey hoisted the American flag. It was a true Norman Rockwell moment, me with my bright red hair and my Cub Scout uniform, saluting the flag as Mickey raised Old Glory.

Also in third grade, I was so in love with Debbie, the prettiest and smartest girl in school, that I decided to give her a ring, a thing so precious in my eyes that I had put it in a plain white envelope and stuck about thirty staples around it, for protection.

When I first saw the ring in a gumball machine at Johnnie's Market, a small grocery store across the street from the school, I wanted it for Debbie. Luckily, my mother was always sending me to the store for cigarettes and giving me a dime for a reward. After handing the *My son has permission to pick up my cigarettes* note to the store owner, I'd run over to the gumball machine, put in my dime, and turn the handle. As each gumball rolled out of the machine, I watched the ring drop closer to the bottom.

Many gumballs later, I ran over to the machine but couldn't see the ring. It was gone! *Someone else must have gotten it.* I was so sad. *Wait! Maybe it's hiding under the gumballs?* I put a dime in the machine and turned the handle while crossing the fingers on my left hand. My purchase rolled down the chute and hit the chrome-plated metal flap. *Ping!* It made a different sound than a gumball. *Could it be?* I opened the flap and out rolled the ring inside a clear plastic ball! I grabbed it and ran toward the door.

"Umm, young man, aren't you forgetting something?" the storekeeper pointed at the cigarettes. I grabbed the cancer sticks and ran home.

"What's this?" Debbie asked as if I was annoying her.

"It's ...uh...uh...a present."

"For what?"

"Uh...j-j-just...uh...a present."

"What are all these *staples* for?"

I stood there gaping.

She opened the envelope with great difficulty, removed the ring, looked at it, put it into her pocket, and didn't say a word. I turned and walked away sheepishly.

Oh, the troubles of a love-struck third grader.

It's probably a good thing nothing came of my advances to Debbie. About fifteen years later, when I was in my biker phase, I saw her at a tavern in Yuba City, snorting white powder off the bar. I heard she spent most of her adult life in a wheelchair and died in her forties.

Chapter Seven
Jell-O Jerky Blues

Several steel poles supported the Linda School corridor roof. There was one that I held onto while Mr. West, my fourth-grade teacher, gave some swift and powerful swats to my backside with his paddle.

I was a star thistle in Mr. West's side during fourth grade because I never did my homework, and as fate would have it, I was in his class again when I advanced from Linda Elementary to Alicia, the middle school in Linda. Mr. West had also transferred to Alicia. Luckily for me, he never used his paddle on my sixth-grade bottom. Somehow, I had become more responsible and less of a troublemaker. I once overheard Mr. West commenting to another teacher about how I had matured.

Lunch was always the best part of the school day, along with Physical Education and recess.

The lunch ladies, their hair tied up in net-covered buns, eyed the motley group of youngsters walking through the line.

Chili Bean Thursday was my favorite lunch day. Chili beans, cornbread, green beans, and Jell-O: in my eyes, a nearly perfect meal, if it weren't for the Jell-O.

The ladies just couldn't get the art of Jell-O making right. There it would sit, a three-inch-square by one-inch-high artificially flavored and colored wobbly glob. No epicurean's dream, even when made properly.

It seemed as if they never let the gelatin dissolve fully before they poured it into the sheet pans because it was nearly impossible to eat the whole piece. After I'd eaten what I could, a nearly one-sixteenth-of-an-inch layer of undissolved gelatin would stick to my lunch tray.

I could see my fellow classmates trying hard to chew this Jell-O Jerky but without much luck. I thought about throwing my piece of the rubber-like substance against one of the windows surrounding the room. Would it stick, like spaghetti? Perhaps my classmates would join me in my Jell-O revolt and throw their pieces against the windows. Soon there could be a multi-colored hue to the room as sunlight filtered through the colored gelatin.

Lacking the courage of a revolutionary, I walked over to the trash can and threw away what remained of my lunch.

In 2005 when I was 50, my sisters and I came back to our alma mater for the school's sesquicentennial (150 year) celebration.

The open field by Linda Elementary is almost gone now, having been filled with new buildings, parking lots and so-called temporary classrooms.

For the sesquicentennial, the multi-purpose room had been decorated with streamers, balloons, and pictures from the past. A video of memorable school activities played on a monitor. What appeared to be current and former teachers chatted at a table. As each person walked into the room, you could see the teachers looking them over, perhaps trying to recognize a former student. I didn't recognize any of the teachers. They looked too young to have taught me.

I walked over to the yearbook table and looked for the years when I attended Linda Elementary but couldn't find anything.

"Your yearbooks are probably over there with the black-and-white ones," a young Asian woman suggested.

"Do I look that old?"

"Uh, sorry."

At the old people's table, I discovered my fourth-grade yearbook and opened it. I found my class and looked at the black-and-white images of former classmates. Turning the pages, I searched for people in different grades and classes and recognized Debbie, Mickey, and others.

Some of them were still in the area and seemed to be doing fine and leading successful lives.

But some had already passed on, like Debbie, I assumed from drugs or alcohol. Some had been in prison. I felt sad for the difficulties many of them endured and might continue to endure. But I also felt grateful for my life.

Leaving the room, I walked over to a concession stand and bought a hotdog.

From a small bench I looked out into the courtyard of my former school. Adults and children laughed and smiled as they visited classrooms together. Most appeared to be of Hmong descent, new immigrants who escaped the hill country of Laos to come to America, not unlike many parents of my former classmates who were economic refugees from America's dust bowl. All in search of a better life.

The celebration was almost over. A young man was cleaning the concession stand, banners came down, the crowds thinned, and my sisters walked by and said they were leaving.

As I got into the car and we drove away, I was still thinking about the photos in the yearbook.

"You're awfully quiet," my sister Mary commented to break the silence.

"Yeah, I was just wondering what happened to all those people we knew at school. And how little we really know about others."

Chapter Eight

Backyard Gold

Tom Sawyer had his caverns. Huck Finn had the Mississippi River. I had the Yuba Goldfields.

The Yuba Goldfields, also known by locals as the Dredger Ponds, is an otherworldly landscape of nearly ten thousand acres of rock and gravel piles between the towns of Smartsville and Marysville, along the Yuba River in California. Huge dredgers floated in diverted river water and lumbered forward digging up the virgin earth to search for gold. It was an environmental nightmare that created over two hundred emerald-colored ponds.

But nature can be forgiving and tenacious. Cottonwood seeds found dirt next to the ponds, sprouted and grew into magnificent trees. Birds nested in the trees. More vegetation grew. Fish flourished. Beavers, muskrats, coyotes, snakes, otter, deer, mountain lions and other wildlife returned. Waterfowl discovered the ponds, as did a nature-lover from Minnesota and his son.

I first remember driving a few miles from our house with my dad to the end of Brophy Road where we'd park and walk past the *No Trespassing* sign into the dredger ponds. It wasn't a long walk.

"I've been here already with Frank from work. He caught a nice bass in that one there," Dad explained as we walked past a long narrow pond.

"How come we don't fish there?"

"There's a large pond further up. I'd like to try that one."

I scurried over to a small concrete structure with a cave-like opening sitting near the road.

"Can I go inside?"

"Probably not a good idea. Might be wasps or black widows in there. Or even worse, a rattlesnake. See look. There's a rattlesnake skin right here."

I looked at the paper-thin skin and bent down to carefully pick it up. As I held it in my hands, I wondered where its former owner might be. *Inside the concrete cave? Underneath those nearby rocks?* I gently blew the skin off my hands. The wind carried it to a patch of star thistles where it stuck, then fluttered in the spring breeze. A curious hawk eyed us from a cottonwood tree and flew away.

Before long, we were at the large pond. My dad set down his tackle box, grabbed the end of the long bamboo pole he was carrying and tied some clear line to it. He then added a hook and bobber to the line and baited the hook with a worm.

"We'll get you started first. I'll toss this out and you hold the pole. If you see the bobber go down, yank the pole and see if you can catch something."

He gave me the pole and I stared at the red and white bobber. Within seconds it was moving. With all the might of a seven-year-old, I jerked the pole. Nothing! No fish. No worm.

"You jerked too hard. Next time be patient. Let 'em take the hook, then jerk softly to set it. Then bring it in."

My dad re-baited the hook, tossed the line into the water and handed me the pole. Again, seconds later, the bobber bobbed. I did as he said. Soon I caught my first fish ever, a three-inch-long bluegill.

"Great job! Too small for eating, but we can save it for fertilizer. When we get home, I'll plant some corn and put that fish next to it like the Indians taught the Pilgrims. Now you've gotta learn how to bait your own hook and cast your line."

After several attempts I got the hang of it. Before long, I had caught at least ten fertilizer-sized bluegill and wanted to take a break. I wanted to go exploring.

"Can I climb that pile of rocks to see what's on the other side?" I asked, pointing to the small hill next to the pond.

"Sure. Looks safe enough. Just don't get out of my sight."

I ran over to the rocks and began my ascent. The climb was more difficult than expected. The rocks were round and loose and would slide as I stepped on them. But I continued onward and upward. About halfway up the hill I stopped and looked down at my dad moving his fly rod back and forth, then softly casting a home-tied artificial fly onto the pond. A fish took the bait and splashed. He reeled it in then saw me looking and held up the large bluegill for me to see. It was a *lot* bigger than the ones I caught. I gave him a thumbs up then continued my journey upward.

Finally, I made it to the top and could now see another pond below me on the other side. Startled mud hens scurried off. A beaver flapped its tail against the water with a loud *plop!* and swam away. I could see orchards near where my dad had parked. Far away sat a dredger. I watched a plane descend towards Beale Air Force Base and heard a faint roar. Around me, as far as I could see, were rock piles and ponds. I had entered a magical place that would become my playground for years. A place for adventure, a place of solitude and contentment.

Chapter Nine
A Bountiful Day

"**Ai**n't nobody gonna pick us up," Mickey complained, still holding up his thumb. Another car approached as we walked west along Hammonton/Smartsville Road toward Griffith Ave. "Who's gonna want us in their car? It's been rainin' since we left the dredger and we're soaked."

"You're prob'ly right. I wouldn't pick up wet kids carryin' guns either. Specially if I saw 'em with a stringer of fish and a dead duck," I responded as I held up our bounty for the motorist to see.

"And I wouldn't take a ride from you. You're only thirteen and don't have a driver's license."

"Ha, ha. Good one."

The startled lady sped by.

"Yeah. But maybe a farmer will give us a ride in the back of his pickup?" I pondered. "Look. There's a truck coming now."

We both thrust out our thumbs as I held my .22 rifle between my legs and Mickey held his shotgun between his.

The farmer drove by shaking his head.

My friend was right. No one picked us up on our over five-mile trek from the ponds to my home in Linda.

As we walked down the dirt road toward the house, I heard our Labrador mutt, Charcoal, barking, then looked across the field and saw Dad come out to watch us from the front porch.

He can probably hardly see us. It's almost dark.

As a bolt of lightning flashed near Olivehurst, I started counting, "One Mississippi, two Mississippi..."

"Whatcha doin'?" drawled Mickey.

"...three Mississippi, four Mississippi, five Mississippi."

Boom!

"Wow! That thunder was sure loud."

"That's because the lightning was only about a mile away. That's why I was counting. Sound travels at about five miles a second."

"That's interesting. How you know that?"

"My grandpa taught me when I was at his cabin in Minnesota. There's a lot of thunderstorms there during the summer."

Seconds after hearing the thunder we were walking in a torrential downpour.

"Let's make a run for it!" Mickey yelled.

"Why bother? We're already soaked and besides, I'm beat. We're almost there anyways. Look, here comes Charcoal running up to meet us."

As we approached the house, I could see Dad puffing a cigarette and holding a can of Hamm's beer, *From the Land of Sky-Blue Waters.*

"You boys are quite the sight," Dad said with a grin as we walked onto the porch. "You got quite a haul there. Who shot the duck?"

"I did. Mickey also shot a jackrabbit with my .22. We left it for the buzzards."

"My, my. A couple o' sharpshooters. Put your catch and that duck in the laundry sink and take off your wet clothes. You can hang 'em up near the wood stove. I'll grab you some shorts. There's some chili simmerin' on the stove. Bet you're both hungry."

"Are we ever."

After changing into my blue jean cutoffs, we hung up our wet clothes near the Franklin wood burner, then huddled next to it, shivering.

"Here's some hot cocoa to get you warm. I'll grab some bowls and cornbread, then you boys can serve yourselves some of that chili."

"Thanks Mr. Gauper. Those beans sure smell good. I can hardly wait to have some."

After drinking our cocoa, we served ourselves some chili and sat in silence savoring our hot meal. I looked at Mickey. He was <u>so</u> skinny. No wonder his shotgun always nearly knocked him down whenever he shot it. I thought back to when he and I shot our first pheasant together.

It was the previous year, after we had both passed our Hunter's Safety Course and went on our first hunt together. We had just hopped a barbed-wire fence after walking through an irrigated pasture near our property when we spooked it.

I took the first shot and hit it! We rushed over to the downed pheasant, but it flew away again. It was now Mickey's turn. *Bam!* He fired and almost fell over but hit the bird. Now it was dead. We proudly carried our prize back home for Dad to see. We were so pleased with ourselves.

The next day, I made two pheasant sandwiches from a loaf of Russian black bread Dad found in the dumpster behind the Wentz grocery store. I offered one to Mickey during lunch at Alicia school.

"Black bread! That's weird. Bread's sposed to be white, like this." He held up his Wonder Bread and bologna sandwich.

Several boys gathered round and watched in awe as I consumed my gourmet fare.

"Where'd you get pheasant?"

"Mickey and I shot it."

"Both of you?"

"Yep."

"What's it taste like?"

"Pheasant."

"What you spittin' out?"

"Bird shot. I have another sandwich if anyone wants it."

They shook their heads.

"What's so funny?" Mickey asked as he ate his last bite of chili.

"Oh, I was just thinkin' about that pheasant we shot together. You never got to eat any of it. I offered you a sandwich at school, but you didn't want it."

"I wasn't 'bout to eat no nigga bread."

"Don't you dare talk like that in this house, young man," Mom scolded from her perch on the couch as she exhaled a cloud of cigarette smoke.

"Sorry 'bout that, Mrs. Gauper."

"Apology accepted," Mom replied as she shuffled her cards for another round of solitaire and dropped a cigarette butt into an empty beer-can on the coffee table.

"You want the duck?" I asked Mickey.

"Naw! I don't think Ma'll know how to cook it. How's about I take the catfish? She knows how to cook 'em. My brothers are always catchin' 'em. You keep the crappie and bluegills."

"Okay."

"Boy, this chili's delicious. It was sure a good ideal for your dad to make it. It's the best I've had."

"Don't you mean idea?"

"Yeah. That too."

"Mr. Gauper, thanks for making this. Do you mind if I have some more? Sure's good."

"Have as much as you'd like. You're cold and hungry. 'Bout anything would taste good right now. I'm leavin' to the store in half an hour. I can give you a ride home."

We finished eating, grabbed our almost dry clothes and headed to the laundry room to get dressed. We removed all the fish from the stringer, then re-strung the five catfish for Mickey to take home.

"You boys ready? I'm headin' out. Mickey, throw your fish in the back of the truck. Don't forget your shotgun."

We ran through the rain to Dad's pickup.

"Since you've got the gun, you ride shotgun," I chuckled as I hopped into the cab. "You have to roll down the window to open the door when you get out. The inside handle's busted."

"Where'd you catch your fish?" Dad asked as he drove through the large mud puddle that was as wide as the dirt road.

"We caught all the crappie and some bluegills at the Dantoni pond. The catfish are from a pond near the river where I shot the duck," I answered.

"You did some serious walkin'. Bet you'll sleep well tonight."

When we reached a ramshackle house on Hammonton Road, Dad stopped. Mickey rolled down the window to open the door.

"Thanks for the ride, Mr. Gauper. See you at school tomarrah, Wobert."

He grabbed his fish from the truck bed, and I rolled the window back up.

As I watched my friend walk down a path to the backyard with his shotgun on his shoulder and a stringer of well-earned fish, I never imagined how different our future paths would be. Mickey would spend most of his life in and around Linda, whereas mine would be elsewhere. He'd get shot and lose his leg after robbing a liquor store, while I was busy trying to save the world.

Dad drove to the store for another six-pack of Hamm's.

Chapter Ten

Peaches and Creatures

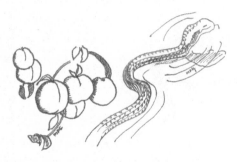

Mickey and other friends, like Matt, continued to visit the dredger ponds with me. We would often walk or ride our bicycles to the end of Griffith, across Hammonton/Smartsville Road, down a gravel road by Lewis's Dairy, along a levee, then past a peach orchard.

I first met Matt when he joined our Senior Little League baseball team, after moving to Olivehurst with his family from Oklahoma. He spoke with a strong Southern accent and was tall and lanky, with black hair and a slightly dark complexion. We were both in our early teens.

"My dad's part Cherokee and still lives in Oklahoma," Matt drawled one scorching summer day while we were walking to the ponds and stopped to pick some ripe peaches from a nearby tree.

"Who's that guy that comes with your mom to our games?"

"That's my stepdad. How much longer 'till we go swimmin'? I'm burnin' up."

"Not much longer. See that pile of rocks? There's a long, narrow pond nearby where we can stop for a swim." We were about to hop a barbed-wire fence into the dredger ponds.

After a brief swim and some sweet juicy cling peaches, Matt was skipping rocks, while I was sitting in the shade of cottonwoods, watching ants attack our discarded peach pits with the ripe flesh still clinging to them.

Suddenly, birds in a nearby tree squawked loudly. Then we heard the strangest noise. It was a sound I had never heard before, like the high-pitched screaming of an animal. But I didn't see any around. The eerie noise appeared to be coming from under a leaf-covered tree limb, just above the water, about fifty yards away, and echoing off the rock piles. We looked at each other with bewilderment.

"Whatcha think that is?" Matt whispered.

I shrugged my shoulders. "Let's check it out."

We cautiously swam toward the commotion of faint splashing and what sounded like shrill groaning. As we neared the shoreline, we propelled ourselves forward by pushing off from submerged rocks with our feet and hands. The noise grew louder and louder as we floated silently closer. Then I saw the source of the spine curling shrills.

"It's a snake!" I murmured.

"A snake? Y'all got screamin' snakes in California?"

"I don't think so. Look. There's something in its mouth."

We moved closer. Barely visible in the jaws of the snake was the mouth of a screaming frog! Wide-eyed, we watched in horror as the reptile took one last swallow of the unfortunate amphibian. There was a final muffled scream, then abrupt silence as the satiated snake swam away.

"That's the creepiest thing I ever saw in my life! I'm gonna have screamin' frog nightmares!"

"Me too. Maybe we'll have mental problems. Do you think people will believe us when we tell 'em what we saw?"

"Don't matter. We both saw *and* heard it. Where we goin' next?"

"We'll go to the Dantoni pond. There's something I want to show you."

After about a half-hour trek down a gravel road and over several rock piles, we passed about twenty drying garments spread out against a mound of rocks.

"Those are from the Mexican farm workers who live in trailers nearby. They wash their clothes in the pond. My dad and I see them sometimes. I used to be kinda scared of them 'til Dad asked them for a jump-start for his truck and they were pretty helpful. He sometimes gives them fish he caught."

"Do they soak it in lime juice and eat it raw? I heard that's what Mexicans do. How much further?" Matt asked impatiently.

"We're here. Head up that path next to the clothes."

After walking up the trail we looked down at the small lake and I pointed toward a tiny stand of trees.

"Follow me," I told Matt as I waded into the water. He followed me as I plodded through reeds and cattails toward a large bush, where I had hidden something special.

"Here it is. A raft my neighbor Tommy and I made from railroad ties we found nearby. We scrounged up nails and rope to put it together. We use those loose boards sitting on top as paddles. I've got an exciting story to tell about the first time we used it."

"Hope it don't include no screaming frogs!"

Ribbit. A nearby frog agreed.

"Nope. Let's untie it and float it further out. I'll tell you my story while we're sitting on it. It'll be more dramatic."

We hopped aboard and paddled our vessel to mid-pond.

"So, what's the story?" Matt asked while he sat at the opposite end of the raft, his feet dangling in the water.

"Well, Tommy and I were fishing off the raft, on its maiden voyage, a little further out than we are now. We saw this huge blob or shadow moving around underneath us. I thought it might be our own Loch Ness Monster or something."

Matt quickly pulled his legs out of the water.

"Suddenly my fishing rod started bending. I was afraid to reel my pole in. No tellin' what was at the end of the fishing line. I reeled it in anyways. But instead of the Loch Ness Monster or other fearful creature, I'd hooked a nice-sized crappie. Tommy also had one. That blob must've been a school of crappie! We caught at least twenty fish that day."

"That's it? My dad and I used to see and catch lots of crappie in Oklahoma. All this swimmin' and walkin's made me tired and hungry. We shoulda packed a lunch. I'd like to lay down and work on my tan."

"You already got a tan. But go ahead. Watch out for splinters. I'll swim back to shore and sit in the shade to work on not gettin' a sunburn. Don't spend too long out here though. You never know, there might be a creature lurking underwater after all."

That ought to make him nervous, I chuckled as I swam to a tree with a rope swing.

From my spot in the shade, I threw twigs into the water and watched as small perch swam to the splashes. Mexican voices came from nearby and two men carried clothes to the shoreline. It was the guys that had helped my dad start his truck. They saw Matt lying on the raft, then nervously peering into the water. Then they recognized me and waved.

I'd a mind to sneak off and leave Matt there working on his suntan. He wouldn't have a clue how to get back home. He'd have to ask those Mexicans for help.

The farmworkers started singing while washing their clothes as a chorus of frogs seemed to join in. I chuckled and remembered when my little sister, Mary, was sitting at this same spot and had burped loudly. What sounded like hundreds of frogs responded to what they must have thought was a mating call.

"Maybe they think you're their queen? Better not burp again, or there might be a frog stampede," I teased.

"Bob! Bob!" Matt was shouting from the raft and waving.

He must be too scared to get in the water. Guess I have to swim out there and help him.

"You paddle on the right, and I'll push the raft while I'm swimming," I told Matt when I arrived. In a short while, we had the raft hiding in the reeds and tied up to the bush.

We smelled smoke and roasting tortillas. The farmworkers had started a small fire next to the lake.

"God I'm hungry. We're headin' back soon I hope."

"Yeah, we'll head back. There's a shortcut through a prune orchard we can take."

As we walked through the orchard, we could still smell the roasting tortillas.

"We shoulda asked them fellas for some food. Betcha they woulda fed us," Matt whined.

"Maybe so. Doubt they have much to spare though. Why don't you eat some prunes?"

"Naw. They give me the shits."

I'm not sure what happened to Matt. I don't remember him in high school. I believe he moved back to Oklahoma, which was a good thing. He once encouraged me to shoplift candy bars from the Yuba Market in Marysville and we were both busted. Police also caught us sneaking into the Marysville Drive-In on Erle Rd.

What really bothered me was how he liked breaking things. I could understand stealing stuff or trying to watch movies for free. But vandalism made no sense. Thankfully, we parted ways before he could lead me further down a path of crime.

Thirty years after my experiences with Matt at the dredger ponds, I visited a shop at the end of Dantoni Rd. to inquire if they'd like to have a 7up vending machine installed. While chatting with the elderly man, I mentioned my days of raft-building and catching crappie in the nearby pond. He looked at me with surprise.

"That's private property. I planted them crappies. You helped build that raft, outta my railroad ties? I was always tryin' to catch them thieves."

He did not want a vending machine.

Chapter Eleven

The Dirt Road

What's that sound? I wondered, as I walked home one early summer day after Little League practice. It was faint, but as I stopped and listened, I could hear a whimper coming from the cornfield next to the dirt road that led to our house.

Hopping the barbed wire fence, I made my way through the field toward the whimpering. As I approached the sound, several cornstalks began to rustle briskly. I stopped, using both arms to cautiously part the giant stalks, and discovered a young black Labrador dog whose leash was tangled in the field corn. It was sure glad to see me. As I tried to free it, the dog kept jumping around, wagging its tail, and licking my face. Finally, I opened the clasp on the leash and the puppy darted away down a narrow path between the high corn rows, stopping briefly to look back at me and wag its tail a few more times.

That dirt road has a signpost now: *Tiptoe Lane*. Although it had no name when I was growing up, some of the locals called it Gauper Lane because we lived at the end. A former volunteer with the Linda Fire Department remembers that their map once listed it as *Gauper Lane*. Too bad the name didn't stick; having a road named after our family would have been an honor, even if it was only dirt.

Tiptoe Lane is perpendicular to Griffith Ave., parallel to Hammonton and Beale Roads in Linda. It's about a quarter of a mile long and, as dirt roads go, has never been in the best of shape. During my childhood it was scarred with potholes which filled with water during the rainy season.

About two-thirds of the way up, where the road made a ninety degree turn to the left, an especially large hole obstructed the entire bend. When that hole was full of water it was nearly impossible, even for the most intrepid dirt road navigator, to continue down the lane on dry land.

For pedestrians there was some relatively dry ground next to the fence where a person could hold onto the fence, and carefully side-step to the corner post. Once you made it to the post, you could grab it with one hand, then swing your body around the corner.

One frosty morning I was in a hurry to catch the school bus, so I quickly scuttled along the fence line, carefully grabbed the post (making sure my manhood didn't smash against it) and swung my leg around; but when my foot hit the frozen grass, it slipped, and I fell backwards. *Plop!* I landed in the large pothole, now a frigid mud puddle, while thin pieces of ice floated around me. I didn't know if I should laugh or cry, but in any case, I missed the bus.

There were good points about living at the end of a dirt road. We always knew when someone was coming to visit. Our dogs would bark, and if the corn wasn't too tall, you could look out across the field and decide which course of action to take. If we didn't recognize the vehicle, it was usually the Jehovah's Witnesses and we had time to run and hide. Likewise, if it was Mormon missionaries on their bicycles, sometimes I would climb out a back window to avoid them.

You got a lot of exercise walking to the bus stop or visiting a friend's house. If we got a ride home from someone, since most people didn't want to get their cars dirty, they'd usually drop us off where the dirt road met the pavement. (Speaking of dirt meeting pavement, my wife says that sounds like a good metaphor for our marriage, but that's another story.)

Attempts at keeping our own vehicles clean were futile. I found it especially challenging to maintain the shiny chrome of my chopped Triumph motorcycle. I should have stuck with the '63 Volkswagen Beetle my sister sold me.

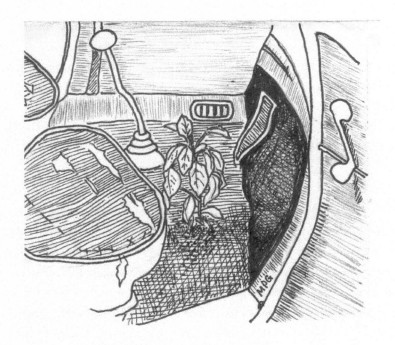

The Beetle was a faded red color that complemented its rust spots. The floorboards were especially rusty, and you could see the ground in some places. Dust and water would creep through the floor and somehow a weed seed found its way into the passenger side, sprouted, and started growing. I grew fond of that plant and would admonish passengers to take care around my unique vehicle accessory. Sadly, the car-plant started dying as summer approached and the mud puddles on the road dried up. I briefly contemplated prolonging its life with supplemental watering; but it was getting big and I didn't want to risk explaining to a police officer what was growing in my car. So I let my plant friend dry up and die a natural death, which didn't take long, since the summer sun made the inside of that Volkswagen like an oven.

I considered removing the caked dirt from the floorboards after that foray into mobile horticulture; but as I was about to, I noticed I could no longer see the ground. My

Volkswagen Bug now had custom-made adobe flooring which I chose to keep. Bet you won't find that in J.C. Whitney's automotive accessory catalog.

My life has been like a dirt road, with at least a fair share of potholes and mud puddles. Yet here I am, still surviving, some (like my wife) would say *thriving,* in spite of adversity. She says my soul is lined with rock-solid adobe, from decades of dust and dirt.

And maybe a little pig manure...

Chapter Twelve

Pig Stories

Then, there was Oinky.

Pigs are smart. Oinky was especially so. My dad could never keep her penned up.

"I should've named her Houdini. Or better yet, I shouldn't have named her at all. Harder to turn 'em into dinner once you've named 'em," my dad said one afternoon after a useless attempt to cage the intrepid piglet.

But who could blame her? Who would stay all alone in a stinky pen, when there was acreage to explore, a cat and dog to play with and children to accompany, down a dirt road to the bus stop?

Oinky never walked with me or my brother to the bus stop. She preferred my sisters.

She'd wait in the early morning near the front porch steps for them to leave the house, and off she'd go with the two girls, down the road past the large fig tree on the left where the road made a sharp turn (where I fell into the mud puddle), past the neighbors' ramshackle barn and house to Griffith Avenue, where two young girls and a pig would wait for a school bus.

Once my sisters were safely on the bus and it had driven away, Oinky would trot back home alone.

Joining my sisters on their walk to meet the school bus was interesting enough, but Oinky would also meet them at the end of the dirt road after school.

"Don't know how that pig did it," my dad recalled years later. "She didn't even have a watch."

Maybe it was the sound of the bus dropping off kids at Alberta and Hammonton Road? Maybe she had some type of internal clock? I don't know. But somehow, she knew when the girls were coming home. She'd scurry off down our road to Griffith and wait for a short time 'til the bus came. Then she'd join the girls for the walk back.

I don't know what eventually happened to Oinky. I'm sure she never ended up in <u>our</u> freezer as ham hocks, pork roasts, ribs, and sausage. Those items were in the freezer due to insider information that my dad used to "win" a butchered hog from Montgomery Ward's Guess-the-number-of-jelly-beans-in-the-piggy-bank Contest. But that's another story.

My guess is that she was sold to a neighbor, Mr. McRee, who raised pigs next to our property.

"Sooey, sooey!" called McRee to his pigs; and those are the only words I remember him ever saying. He was a quiet man. However, his wife made up for his reticence. She'd often phone our house to talk to my parents about who knows what.

"Uh-huh, yep, uh-huh," my dad kept repeating into the phone's hand piece. "Uh-huh, yep, uh-huh."

One time my dad quietly laid the handpiece on the counter, and as he silently walked away to the bathroom, she continued to jabber. A short while later, he returned and picked up the phone again.

"Uh-huh, yep, uh-huh."

Mr. McRee had a relative who worked at a fruit-packing shed and every summer a dump truck arrived weekly, excreting its cargo of honeydew melons, plums, and various culled fruits for the pigs to eat. Those piles were close to our house, and before long the smell of rotting fruit mixed with the odor of pigs with the runs would fill the summer air.

One summer day while walking home as a young teenager, I heard a strange noise coming from a rickety floorless shed the pigs used for shelter on McRee's property.

"Rrrrgh! Rrrrgh!"

What could that be? A coyote? A mountain lion eating a pig? A pig giving birth?

"Rrrrgh! Rrrrgh!"

Curiosity and concern drove me to investigate the strange sounds from the shed.

I cautiously climbed over the barbed wire fence then grabbed a large oak tree branch for a weapon. I crept closer, carefully avoiding stepping on rotten fruit or pig manure.

"Rrrrgh! Rrrrgh!"

The sound grew louder. My hands began to shake.

"Rrrrgh! Rrrrgh!"

I held my breath and gently placed my eye to a knothole in the shed wall.

I gasped in astonishment. It was McRee taking a crap... a sight I wish I could forget. A red-faced, constipated, skinny old man with his trousers down to his ankles, straining to relieve himself. Too bad *he* didn't eat more fruit.

I visited the old neighborhood many years later. Our humble dwelling at the end of the dirt road is no longer there; the neighbors' barn and house have been replaced by a couple of newer homes, and an almond orchard has been planted nearby. However, the fig tree is still there, and so are the memories.

Chapter Thirteen

I want Jesus on my team!

My middle school, Alicia Intermediate, sat at the intersection of Alicia Avenue and Pasado Road in Linda. It was demolished in 2013 because of its proximity to the airport and a natural gas line. There is now an open field where the school used to be.

I still remember what it was like to attend classes for weeks with a deep pain in my heart because I thought my dad had left the family. His in-laws were visiting, and he was tired of their nagging, so he disappeared for a while. Thankfully, once they departed, he returned. But I knew that wasn't the case for many of my fellow classmates. Maybe that's why Billy was a bully, maybe he couldn't get over his dad leaving and never coming back.

Billy was my friend for a short while, but something changed. For whatever reason, he started picking on me in Woodshop. He made fun of things I was making or threw small pieces of wood at me when the teacher wasn't looking. There wasn't much to Billy, he was short and skinny, so I wasn't afraid of him; but he was *so* annoying. I thought about punching it out with him, but I was worried I might accidentally hit his teeth that stuck out so much and were spaced so far apart he could have flossed with shoelaces. I also didn't want to get in trouble for fighting. But still, going to Woodshop, a class I enjoyed, was taxing. I had to do something, but what? I needed a miracle. That miracle came when I met Jesus.

There it was, written on the blackboard amongst all the other names...*Jesus*. I looked around the room of my seventh-grade Physical Education class but didn't see anyone that looked like Jesus.

The teacher had written the names on the chalkboard so that he could organize soccer teams. *I want Jesus on my team*, I thought, half-praying as the teacher wrote numbers next to the names. I got the number three, and so did Jesus. *He's on my team!* But when his name was called, the teacher pronounced it differently than I had ever heard: "Hey-Zeus."

Hey-Zeus wasn't what I expected, he was a stocky Mexican kid who struggled with English, but he sure knew how to play soccer! It was on the soccer field where the accident happened.

Billy the bully, who was on the opposing team, ran toward the soccer ball as Jesus and I hurried toward him from opposite sides. Billy was aiming for the goal! The three of us kicked toward the ball but Billy kicked it a split-second before us. *Goal!*

But Billy didn't get to see it. He was writhing in pain on the ground. Jesus and I had missed the ball and kicked Billy's leg, both of us at the same time. Somebody called the school nurse and Billy was carried from the field on a stretcher. Surprisingly, I felt sorry for him, much as I had sincerely longed to inflict pain on him in the past. After that, for some reason he never bothered me again.

Someone else of Mexican descent had helped me a year before, in sixth grade, in the boys' bathroom, where middle-school conflicts often take place. I had walked in there after lunch to take a leak and as I was finishing my business, an older student asked me if he could borrow my comb. *Yuck!* I thought, as I looked at his greasy hair. But I wasn't about to tell him no. I handed him my comb and cringed as he combed his hair. The Fonzi wannabe then took my comb and threw it in the unflushed urinal in front of me.

Then suddenly the bully's smirk turned to a look of dismay as Alex, a fellow sixth grader, walked in. Now Alex was no ordinary sixth grader. He was feared by many and had older brothers who were feared even more. He also had a girlfriend who was in the eighth grade.

I watched in amazement as Alex swiftly assessed the situation and flew into action. He grabbed the trembling eighth grader by the front of his shirt collar and held him against a bathroom stall.

"When I let go of you, I want you to grab that comb, comb your hair, wash it off, and then give it back to my friend Bobby. You got that?"

The shocked older boy nodded. When he was let go, he meekly walked over to the urinal, grabbed my comb, shook off some of my pee, and combed his hair. He then rinsed off the comb, wiped it with a towel and handed it to me. Dumbfounded, I took it back.

The school bell rang for the end of lunchtime, and we returned to our classrooms. From my desk, I glanced around to where Alex was sitting. Noticing I was looking at him, he smiled a quick smile and nodded his head slightly.

None of the older students ever bothered me after the bathroom incident. I guess the word had gotten out that I was, indeed, Alex's friend.

Chapter Fourteen
Gatekeeper

"How'd yer dad get that key?" Mickey's brother Lenny asked me after he had driven through the gate I had opened for him.

"They made him an honorary game warden after he turned some people in for shootin' beavers. Told him to report trespassers and illegal huntin'."

"Wow. That's neat. Bet not many people have that. Whenever we wanna come out to the ponds, we'll have to invite you."

I was special. My dad had a key to the gates at the dredger ponds and he let me use it. The beat-up station wagon was packed with me, Mickey, his four older brothers and their friend Teddy. I got to sit next to the front passenger door because I had my dad's key.

"Where we headin'?" I asked Lenny as he guided his car down the gravel road.

"We're goin' to the dredger. We sometimes walk to it, but it's a long walk. Some of us might go swimmin'."

Swimming in February? It was a nice sunny day, but that water would be cold. Really cold. Not sure if I wanted to do that. But my dad's friend Ralph, a security guard for the ponds who once also taught school in Hammonton, used to live on the dredger and went swimming every day. I still remembered overhearing a conversation between Ralph and Dad.

"Yep. Dove into the pond with a bar of soap every morning. Even through the winter. Jumped from a ledge near my room. Better than coffee for waking up. I'd still be teaching school if the bourgeoisie wouldn't have fired me because of my political views," Ralph said one evening after too many beers at our house.

"And for teaching them at the school," my dad piped in.

"Yeah. That wasn't too smart. But someone has to speak up for the worker."

The dredger came into view as we skidded around a sharp corner. I was excited. I'd seen the dredger from a distance and always wanted to see it up close.

Lenny stopped in a cloud of dust next to the dredger.

It was huge. About half the size of a football field, it looked like a floating industrial two-story building, sitting on a huge barge, with cranes at both ends. Cables and winches were everywhere.

"How do ya think it works?" I asked Mickey after we got out of the car.

"Looks like those big buckets in front dig into the ground like a huge chainsaw. After takin' gold out, they leave the rocks along the shoreline. That's why there's rock piles everywhere."

I wondered if this was the dredger Ralph used to live on. *Were there more dredgers? Where was his room? Where did he jump from?* I chuckled at the mental image of Ralph, a muscular, slightly overweight bald guy, diving into the pond naked.

"Lenny and Teddy like to jump from that walkway near that crane," said Mickey as he pointed upward.

"How high do you think that is?"

"Not sure. Maybe sixty feet or so. I once went up there and looked down. Too high for me. No way was I gonna jump. You like jumpin' from high places like Beale Falls and the train trestle. Maybe you should join 'em."

"Maybe. Looks a lot higher than that trestle over the river to Marysville. But I'll check it out."

Soon all seven of us had made our way to the deck of the dredger.

"Who besides Teddy's gonna join me and jump from the walkway?" Lenny shouted as he stripped to his Fruit of the Looms. "We'll be the first ones to go swimmin' this year."

The brothers quietly shook their heads.

"I'm game," I recklessly exclaimed.

"You sure? It's pretty scary up there." Mickey looked concerned.

I nodded yes.

I undressed and followed Lenny and Teddy as they climbed the stairs next to the metal building, then along a steel walkway and up some more stairs. We climbed higher and higher.

Lenny stopped along the way and pointed down to where metal buckets were partially submerged in the water.

"See them catfish? I'm gonna try catchin' 'em once we've jumped. Almost there."

I looked to the water far below.

What was I thinking? I was just showing off. It was a lot higher than I thought. But I couldn't back down now, they'd think I was a sissy.

Finally, we made it to our jumping off point.

"Nice view, ain't it?" said Teddy as we stood there in our skivvies.

The view *was* nice, but I was too nervous to enjoy it.

"How deep is the water?" I asked, trying to hide my jitters.

"Deep enough. I checked it out last year. Couldn't swim to the bottom. They don't use the dredger anymore, so it hasn't moved. Don't think 'bout it too much. Just climb over the railing like this. Stand here and jump! Waaaa!" Lenny screamed as he plunged towards the water.

Plop! His loud splash echoed off the dredger.

"You're next," said Teddy.

Everyone was staring from the deck below as I nervously climbed over the railing. I was shaking and thought about climbing back. But that seemed scarier than jumping. I took a deep breath then leapt.

Before hitting the water, I pointed my feet down and quickly covered my face with my hands. *Plop!* I hit the cold water. It was a good jump. No water up the nose. No stinging on misplaced limbs. The frigid water took my breath away. When I surfaced, I heard clapping and whooping. Strangely, I could hear female voices. I quickly swam to the nearby shoreline and looked up. Two couples were standing high up on the dredger.

The guys were wearing Marysville High School letterman jackets. I was a freshman and recognized them as upperclassmen jocks and cheerleaders.

I was still in the water and freezing.

Great. They're going to see me in my underwear when I get out. Good thing I'm not skinny dipping like Ralph. Teddy must be really embarrassed. They can see him and he probably knows them since they're in the same grade.

Climbing out of the water, I sat down shivering on the rocky shoreline then watched Teddy jump. His extended arms made a loud *splat* as he hit the water.

Ouch! That's not how you do it. He gets a five for dredger jumping. Bad form.

I dove in and swam back to the dredger rather than clambering over the rocks in my soaking wet underwear.

"We didn't think you'd do it! Teddy and Lenny are the only ones that'll jump from there. And you! The rest of us are chicken. I even heard those so-called jocks sayin' it was too high," Mickey explained proudly after I had dressed, and we sat eating our baloney sandwiches.

Chicken, or smart. Not sure I'll ever do that again.

"Look what I caught," said Lenny as he walked up holding a stringer of six nice-sized catfish. "I made a ball of smushed-up bread and used that for bait. I know what I'm havin' for dinner: fried catfish, hushpuppies, coleslaw, and an RC. Who wants to use my pole? I'm gonna eat lunch."

I wanted to go fishing, but I was chewing on the last bite of bait.

"Let me use it," said Mickey as he stood up.

"There's no bread left. What are you going to use for bait?" I asked.

"I got my bait right here in my pocket." He pulled out a can of Vienna Sausage. "You watch. I'll be addin' to that stringer in no time."

Mickey was right. Within minutes of casting his line he had a bite. It was a foot-long yellow cat.

Hmm. That's the only thing I'd use those sausages for. Fish bait. Must be an acquired taste.

"We best get goin'!" Lenny shouted from the shoreline. "I forgot it's potluck tonight at church. I'll throw them fish into the watering trough. They'll stay alive. Guess that fish dinner 'll have to wait 'til tomarrah."

We scrambled to the station wagon.

"Let Robert ride shotgun, he's the gatekeeper," Lenny shouted as he turned the ignition key.

A clicking sound came from underneath the hood.

"Dammit. The battry's dead. Shit!"

"Don't let Pastor Booth hear you talk like that. You'll be puttin' dimes in the cussin' jar," said Charlie from the back.

Without a word, all of us except Lenny jumped out of the car and began pushing. Seconds later he popped the clutch and the old car started. Charlie ran to the wagon and stole my coveted seat.

"You can't sit there. That's Rudolph's spot," Lenny shouted, teasing me about the sunburned nose I got every summer.

Charlie got out of the car and gave me a dirty look.

"Shut the door behind me."

I followed him to the back and watched as he crawled inside and sat next to the spare tire and the live, gulping catfish. I slammed the door then ran to my spot. The jocks and cheerleaders stared as our ragtag group drove away. One of the girls waved shyly. I'm not sure if it was meant for me or Teddy sitting behind me.

"Let's grab the cats," said Mickey when we arrived at his house.

I held the fish while Mickey began filling an old rusty bathtub with water.

"I don't think Charlie likes me," I said.

"Oh, he's just mad cuz he had to sit in the back. Lenny already told everyone you got ta sit shotgun. Charlie's pretty stupid. He's so stupid, he couldn't get a job suckin' farts outta used car seats."

We laughed as Mickey carefully took a catfish off the stringer then placed it in the filled bathtub.

"Don't know why, but catfish live longer than most other fish outta water. You ever heard 'bout them walkin' catfish in Florida? I read 'bout them in the library. Good thing these ain't that kind, they might try walkin' back to the dredger ponds," Mickey chuckled.

"Now that I have this key, we don't have to walk there anymore either."

But we didn't spend much time at the ponds after Spring arrived, because *that* was baseball season.

Chapter Fifteen
Charlie Brown Days

"**H**ey batter, hey batter, hey batter, swing!"

For me, baseball, like life, had its ups and downs. I won, lost, got hurt, emotionally and physically: lost a front tooth, got a huge black eye, and was knocked unconscious by an errant hardball when playing third base.

Every spring I waited anxiously for baseball season to begin, just like Charlie Brown. I loved the smell of recently mown grass, the sight of honeybees in the clover, the sound of the ump yelling, "Play ball!" the feel of breaking in a brand-new leather glove. The rituals, the strategies. The crack (or ding if the bat's aluminum) of the baseball hitting a bat. Players, fans, and coaches arguing with the umpire.

I played high school baseball one year; wanted to play more but wasn't good enough. But not for lack of trying.

I studied books about baseball, rigged floodlights in front of our house so I could practice my fielding skills late at night by throwing balls against the brick planter my dad built, and even tried to make my own pitching machine from a garage door spring I scrounged from the Kwitcherkickin junk yard in Olivehurst.

My pitching machine was an absolute failure.

After assembling a baseball catapult out of the spring, salvaged two-by-fours and an assortment of hinges and other make-do parts, my invention was ready for field-testing. My brother wisely declined my offer to let him be batter.

I drew a strike zone on an old backyard shed with a dirt clod, cocked my contraption, hooked the two-by-four throwing arm with a metal latch, loaded up a baseball and then yanked on a string tied to the trigger.

Wham! The arm lunged forward, hit the crossmember and broke in half, throwing the baseball into the stratosphere, never to be seen again, or maybe into the next-door field chock-full of star thistles. The busted board hit the strike zone cracking several boards on the shed.

Giving up on the pitching machine, I'd often have my brother pitch while I'd catch, and we'd also attempt to throw out imaginary base runners. That paid off.

"Gauper! Go catch!" the high school baseball coach called out one game, jogging me out of my bench-warming daydream, after the regular catcher had difficulty throwing out base stealers.

"Wow, I didn't know you had such a good arm," a teammate exclaimed after he saw me throw out several runners.

I shrugged. "We played Senior Little League together."

"We did? Oh yeah, you're Greg's brother. I forgot he had a brother. How's he doin'?"

"Okay. He's playing Senior League now. He hit two homers over the fence. No one's done that in years."

"He's sure good."

Yeah, yeah, he was *so* good. I'd heard it hundreds of times. It just wasn't fair. My brother was a natural athlete, and I wasn't.

I was nine years old when I first tried out for Little League. Mickey called me the Saturday after tryouts. I could tell he was excited by how fast he was talking.

"I'm on the Zebras with my brother. The coach said they're pickin' teams today. Anyone call you?"

"Nope."

"They should. You're better than a lotta guys."

I hung up, crossed my fingers, and waited anxiously for a phone call. There wasn't one. I cried all day Sunday and dreaded going to school the next day.

Monday morning, when I climbed onto the school bus after it stopped on Griffith Avenue, my heart sank even further. Nearly every boy was wearing a Little League baseball cap with his team's name on it. Jeff, Greg, Lynn, and others. Even Craig, who always struck out, had a cap. He smirked as I walked by. I sat down in an empty seat and stared sadly out the window as the bus lumbered away.

"How come Craig got picked and I didn't?" I complained to Dad later in the week.

"His dad is best friends with the coach," was the reply. Then Dad called his friend Otis, who was also a coach, but he already had too many players. He said lots of kids didn't make teams and encouraged me to try out the following year.

I tried out the next year with no luck. Finally, when I was twelve, I was picked for the Solons, one of the minor league teams for younger, and not-so-good players. I hoped to get picked for the Majors that year but didn't. I was one of only two twelve-year-old players on the minor league teams. Of course, my brother was chosen for the Majors the first time he tried out. He was three years younger than me. How humiliating. Ultimately, I was called up to the Majors to play the last game of my Little League career and ironically, I made the game-winning hit on my very last at-bat.

"You shoulda been on our team longer," someone commented.

That would have been nice.

In my teens I attended church because of baseball.

Mickey and I, and his brothers, went to the Pentecostal church across the street from Linda Elementary on McLaughlin Way. If you didn't attend church at least once a week, you didn't get to play on the church's softball team. That is, unless you were Scotty, who was so good he was offered a baseball scholarship to Arizona State. He always played, church attendance or not.

We went on Wednesday evenings because that was the shortest service. I never felt comfortable there and it all seemed so foreign. Although I did get first place for my costume during a Harvest Festival Halloween alternative.

I dressed as a girl. With my long red hair, everyone said I looked like Margaret from *Dennis the Menace cartoons*. In case the reader is wondering, that was the first and last time I ever wore a dress.

My baseball trajectory seemed to improve when I went on to Senior League (for thirteen-to-fifteen-year-olds). I hoped to make the All Stars when I was fifteen since I had one of the highest batting averages in the league. But that didn't happen.

For much of my childhood and adolescence I felt like Charlie Brown: dedicated, responsible, determined, yet unnoticed and underappreciated, and I even had Charlie's oversized head. I could barely fit a baseball cap over my big skull without extending it out to the largest notch on the adjustable band.

Later in life my hard work paid off. I was often one of the better baseball players in physical education class, on intramural college teams or in recreational games. Some Japanese friends have called me, with genuine admiration, "Bob Ruth."

Something I learned in baseball, may have even saved my life. But more about that later.

Chapter Sixteen

Girding My Loins

"**D**ude. You've got a big-ass hole in your pants!" a fellow student exclaimed as I was hurrying down the hallway, late for my French class at Marysville High.

I stopped, reached round to my backside, felt a large gap in the fabric, then touched my crotch area. More holes. My jeans were falling apart!

Carefully, I walked back toward my motorcycle, stopped at the hallway exit and looked behind me to see shredded pieces of fabric and dust marking my path along the polished hallway floor.

Outside I stared at my Honda 175 and realized the source of my calamity.

The kick-starter was broken, so I always had to push-start it. However, that morning I couldn't get it started because the battery was dead. I had strapped the battery from my dad's truck to my bike seat, ran wires from his battery to the motorcycle, pushed it briefly down the dirt road, jumped onto the bike and started it. I must have spilled acid onto the bike seat before I reinstalled the battery into my dad's truck.

Thankfully, this time the bike started easily, and I began the five-mile journey home as my pants continued to disintegrate. When I got home, I dug some not-too-dirty jeans out of a hamper and changed.

Before driving back to school, I carefully washed and dried the motorcycle seat.

Having effectively re-girded my loins, I sped along Hammonton Rd.

Man, that was close. I could've walked into class or down a crowded hallway with a big-ass hole in my britches. How embarrassing.

Avoiding embarrassment was one of my goals in high school.

My best friend Mickey was no longer around much. He attended W.T. Ellis Continuation School, also known as Hoodlum High, at the corner of Brophy and Hammonton Roads. W.T. Ellis was the *alma mater* of several of his siblings and mine, too.

When I first started at Marysville High, I knew hardly anyone and had few friends.

In Sophomore year a neighbor and fellow student encouraged me to join the wrestling team. Through lots of practice, I became good at it and eventually was appointed team captain. In Senior Year I received a trophy for *Most Varsity Pins.*

Around that time, many of my fellow teammates told me they voted for me for *Most Valuable Wrestler.* At the Winter Sports Banquet I waited anxiously with my dad to be called upon to receive that trophy. My name wasn't called. A popular football jock, who seldom showed up for wrestling practice, got it instead. I tried hard to shrug off the crushing disappointment so my dad wouldn't see how hurt I was. But I think he knew.

In the movie, *Chariots of Fire,* Olympic runner Eric Liddell says, "I believe God made me for a purpose, but he also made me fast."

I also believe God made me for a purpose, but for some reason, he made me *slow.* That's probably why I was okay as a catcher in baseball or why wrestling became my best sport. I didn't have to run fast.

In high school I passed almost every test required to earn the *Presidential Physical Fitness Award,* a nation-wide program to encourage physical fitness in teenagers. But I failed the fifty-yard-dash; Somehow, I just couldn't run fast enough. How was I supposed to fix that? I was in excellent shape; I ran up and down bleacher stairs almost every day for wrestling training. It felt like an injustice.

However, that year I did receive the *Most Dependable Student Chef* award. Dependable, like Charlie Brown. I had enrolled in FEAST (Food Education and Service Training), the chef preparation program, my junior year.

Whenever anyone asked what inspired me to want to become a chef, I'd reply, "My mother."

"Your mother taught you how to cook?" was often the reply.

"No...not really, although she was good at making toast. I learned how to cook so I could feed myself when my dad was away on a job."

Perhaps I wanted to be a chef because I didn't want to be hungry. During the winter, my dad was often without work. Surveying jobs were scarce because of bad weather. More than once, I remember scouring the kitchen looking for something to eat, and all I could find were jars and jars of inedible pickles one of our neighbors had given us. My dad didn't have the heart to tell her how awful they were.

I even remember walking a couple of miles, one foggy night, to the Peach Bowl Country Club to steal oranges off fruit trees, I was so hungry. I'm sure they tasted a lot better than the raw potato I once saw Mickey's brother eating.

In Senior year, through the FEAST program I got a job at Tony's restaurant in Linda, a highly regarded Italian steakhouse. But lost that job when it burned down a couple of years later.

Many of the students in the chef-training program entered a Bay Area culinary contest that year. I coated a cooked chicken with white aspic and decorated it with the help of my artistic mother the night before the contest. In the morning, I opened the refrigerator to retrieve our masterpiece. It was missing a drumstick! It looked as if someone had ripped it off.

It turned out that my brother came home late and ate it. I didn't enter the contest, but maybe I should have. I could have labeled the mangled chicken *Drunk Brother*

Blues. Maybe I would have won something out of sympathy. But that would have been embarrassing.

Girls scared me in high school. I longed to ask Kathy out, or even to the prom. She wasn't as pretty or as popular as her older sister, but I thought she was cute with her slim figure and long black hair. At least she said hi to me occasionally. My friend Benji told me she liked me, but I wasn't sure I believed him. I struggled for weeks to get up the courage to ask her to the prom. One day I approached her in the school hallway.

"Uh... How are you doing?" I began to sweat, and my face felt hot.

"I'm okay," she answered, looking a little perplexed. "Can I help you with something?"

"Uh...never mind." I lost my courage.

I didn't ask her, or anyone else for that matter. If they said no, that would've been too disappointing, *and* embarrassing.

But there were far more serious issues at stake at Marysville High than my personal struggles with girls, peers, battery acid or a chicken without a drumstick.

We had a small minority of Black students, maybe just one or two percent of the student body; I remember a friendly Black girl being in my FEAST class. One day, I was shocked to see The National Guard with riot gear on campus. According to rumor, racial tension was intense between the Blacks and the "cowboys." I didn't know what side to take, if any. Recently, my sister told me, "I remember you supporting the Black students." I'll take her word for it.

People look back at their high school years with different emotions. For some, it was the best years of their lives; for others it was the worst. For me, it was somewhere in between.

Happily, many of my high school experiences paid off later in life.

Shyness around girls sheltered me until I found the love of my life, who's been with me for almost forty years. Wrestling helped me out of more than a few difficult situations.

I still cook, sometimes write about cooking and once taught Mid-westerners how to prepare seafood. And I'll be super careful if I ever need to strap a battery to a motorcycle seat again.

Many years after high school I was behind a bar servicing some equipment at a tavern in Yuba City. Sitting at the bar was a popular former fellow student with a football jock who I assumed was her husband. They didn't recognize me and acted like I wasn't even there. They both had had too much to drink and were arguing openly. She was loudly listing what she felt were his many inadequacies.

He glanced at me with a forlorn look then tottered toward the bathroom.

"Hello," I smiled at her. "We went to high school together."

She stared at me with a quizzical look.

"Oh yeah," she said slowly. "Aren't you Greg's brother?"

Chapter Seventeen
Yuba College

The local community college was less than a mile from my house. At least as magpies fly, or for a young man willing to hop barbed wire fences and walk through a cow pasture and a field of star thistles.

In high school I never thought about attending the local college. I wanted to be a chef. My friend Benji and I were both planning to attend San Francisco City College chef-training program. But he joined the Air Force instead and I kept working as a cook at Tony's, an Italian restaurant in Linda.

After Tony's burned down, a friend found me a job at a fiberglass company in Olive-hurst. I hated it. I worked in the grinding department, grinding fiberglass and breathing fumes and dust all day long. When I wore a dust mask, the old timers teased me. On breaks those same guys smoked unfiltered Camel cigarettes and chewed tobacco. Their spittle was tinted with the color of the fiberglass we were grinding that day. I suspected their lives would be short.

Even after a shower, my skin would twinkle in the sunlight from the embedded fiberglass dust. It itched like hell, even worse than peach fuzz from peach picking.

I need to do something different, I kept telling myself. *Maybe I should attend Yuba College?*

But I doubted myself and I didn't believe I was college material. Countless dozens of times I drove my old truck past the school but couldn't find the courage to drive into the parking lot. That is, until one day when an angle grinder slipped and gouged my leg at work. (I still have the scar.) The next day I signed up for classes and took an aptitude test.

"Bob, it looks like you're a mechanical genius," the guidance counselor told me. "You're weak in math and English, though. You'll have to take remedial classes without credit."

Taking those remedial classes was embarrassing, especially the English class where nearly everyone had English as their second language. Eventually I learned the differences between two, to and too, it's and its, your and you're but still struggle with lay, laid, lie and lain, as do many Americans. However, I persevered and even signed up for a creative writing class.

Most of my classes were enjoyable: sociology, psychology, business, and others. However, I struggled with math. Luckily, my mother patiently helped me pass my first math class. She couldn't save me from one awkward day, however.

"Eww, what's that smell?" someone asked. Other classmates sniffed, then grimaced. People were looking at me. I looked at the bottom of one of my boots and saw cow manure. I must have accidently stepped on a cow patty while rushing to class. I went outside and wiped my boots on some wet grass and dried them with paper towels from the bathroom. Several people giggled as I walked back inside my classroom. Laughing along with them, I was somehow able to shrug off another potentially embarrassing situation.

As my first semester was ending, I read a *Ski Class Starting!* announcement in the college newspaper. Although, during the winter, you could reach the snow in less than an hour's drive from Linda, I had never experienced it. For a nominal fee, the class included bus transportation from Linda to the Boreal Mountain Ski Resort and back, as well as equipment rental and ski lessons. There would be five-day trips altogether and I promptly signed up.

My first snow skiing experience was a complete disaster.

The "snow" was freezing rain that soaked through my down jacket and the cheap ski pants I found at Goodwill. My first lesson was mostly spent struggling to stand back up after falling down on the slippery ice, while elementary school aged kids skied past, giggling. Instead of skiing, I spent most of the day inside the lodge sipping over-priced hot cocoa. Which wasn't all that bad, since over half of the ladies from Yuba were also there and I even talked to some of them.

Our next trip was so different. The day was bright and sunny, I got the hang of sliding down a snow-covered mound with narrow planks strapped to my feet and didn't waste any money on cocoa. In fact, I didn't even stop for lunch, thinking I'd eat my sack lunch on the bus ride home. But that didn't work out, since I'd left my lunch on the bus and everything was frozen.

After skiing season ended, a fellow Yuba College classmate and I organized a co-ed intramural softball team mostly made up of girls we had met in our ski class. The classmate was also a neighbor who lived on Alberta Ave. We called our team the *No Shows* because most of our teammates seldom showed up for practice. Ironically, they *did* show up for games, where our lack of practice earned us the distinction of never winning anything. The only runs we got were when my classmate or I hit a home run. Despite our dismal season, the experience was pleasantly memorable.

In my sociology class I learned a new word: *Weltanschauung*, meaning the worldview of an individual or group. I realized my worldview was expanding. I began to make new friends but still kept in touch with my old friend Mickey. We'd often meet at Alicia School in the evenings to play basketball with his brothers. His mother worked at the school as a janitor and would let us into the multi-purpose room.

Before attending Yuba College one of my main goals in life was to get a job at the Del Pero-Mondon meat-packing plant and save up to buy a Harley motorcycle. I never could manage to get hired at Del Pero, and during my years at Yuba I gave up on the Harley idea. Instead, I started looking at four-year colleges to attend and decided on the University of Nevada at Las Vegas. To afford that, I would need Nevada State residency.

Chapter Eighteen
The Abyss

Titan 1 missile silo, Chico, California, 2013 (U.S. Air Force photo by Senior Airman Allen Pollard/Released)

"**T**itan Missile Declared Obsolete," Dad announced as he read the 1960's headline in the Appeal-Democrat after taking a sip of strong coffee.

"Why'm I even going to work?" he asked glancing at me.

He was a surveyor at the Sutter Buttes missile site and since I wasn't a teenaged know-it-all yet, I didn't have an answer to his question.

Eventually, work at that over forty-million-dollar hole in the ground was stopped and the project was abandoned.

Abandoned or not, it was sure an exciting place to sneak into during the early seventies.

"Okay. Just follow me in the dark. Don't turn on your flashlights until I tell you to," Tom said to me and Jeff after we got out of the car. He had driven us to the Sutter Buttes, locally known as the World's Smallest Mountain Range, and down a dirt road.

We followed him stealthily in the moonlight up an incline and along a paved road past several small concrete structures. We stopped at one of those structures, then stepped through a door into complete darkness.

"Turn your flashlights on," Tom whispered as he shone his light around the small gray concrete room and down a flight of stairs so deep I couldn't see where it ended.

"Follow me," he said as he descended the staircase, his footsteps echoing down the dark abyss. That was the only sound I was aware of, along with the rattling of the unlit Coleman lantern he was carrying, as we walked about ten minutes down the stairs. Finally, Tom stopped and lit the lantern. The light filled a huge circular empty room about the size of Marysville High School's gymnasium. Pipes, wires, pieces of metal and tunnels were everywhere.

"I think this was the power room," Tom pondered.

"The kitchen and Mess Hall are over there," he pointed his lantern toward a doorway.

"We'll head over there next. Before we do, everyone turn off their lights and listen. You never know, there might be someone else down here. Happened to me before. Scared the shit out of me."

We turned off our lights and listened intently. In the leaden blackness I could hear metal creaking, water dripping and my fellow explorers breathing, but no other sounds of human activity.

The darkness was so thick it was almost palpable, and I was feeling a little spooked. I hoped Tom would ask us to turn on our lights soon. Finally, he said, "Lights on. Let's check out the mess hall."

The room was like a large school classroom. A doorway led into another room that must have been the kitchen. There was an opening between the kitchen and the mess hall where food was probably served. I tried to imagine what it must have been like for the airmen living and working in this underground labyrinth.

"Bob. Bob. You okay?" Jeff jogged me out of my trance.

"Just thinkin' about the people that used to live here. Where we goin' next?"

"We're heading to a silo where a missile used to sit. Tom's waiting."

Tom led us to a concrete tunnel about seven feet in diameter and we followed him into the man-made cave. After about five minutes, he stopped and said, "Bob, lift up that grill below your feet."

I obliged, then he reached down and opened a metal box. Inside were several flashlights, matches, cigarette papers, and a small baggie of marijuana.

"That's my secret stash. Don't want to get caught down here without essentials. I practiced finding that grill in the dark and it was fairly easy."

He bent down and grabbed the weed, matches and rolling papers, then closed the box lid and put back the grill.

"We're almost there. Follow me."

In a short while Tom slowed his walking pace then stopped. He shined his light around what appeared to be a huge circular room from my vantage point inside the tunnel.

"Be super careful. We'll take turns using my flashlight. It's the most powerful." He handed the flashlight to me and stepped aside.

The "room" was a huge concrete silo, and I was standing at the edge of it. I moved the flashlight's beam around the structure. It looked to be about fifty feet in diameter. Around sixty feet above me, rusted steel panels covered the silo's roof that must have opened when the missile was ready to launch. I aimed the light downward.

My heart raced as I looked down into the manmade chasm. The powerful flashlight illuminated the concrete cylinder that was over a hundred feet deep. Water was at the bottom. Boards and other debris floated on the water. Thankfully, nothing moved. *Now that would be a place to hide a body,* I told myself as I made mental notes for my Creative Writing class.

"Hey. My turn," said Jeff as he tapped me on the shoulder. I was glad to change places. While Jeff looked around the silo, Tom rolled a joint by the light of the lantern. He lit it, took a puff, then handed it to me as I sat on the tunnel floor.

"You're missing out," Tom mumbled to Jeff.

Jeff turned around, turned off his flashlight, then sat down next to us. Tom extinguished his lantern. The only light was the glow of the marijuana cigarette that shone brighter as someone inhaled the THC-laden smoke. Tom took the last drag then tossed the roach into the darkness. Soon, I heard quiet snoring then looked at my watch. It was nearly 3 a.m.

"Anyone awake?" I whispered.

Silence.

I leaned against the wall of the concrete tunnel and joined them in their slumber.

"Wake up! We've gotta get the hell out of here! The sun's coming up soon and we might get caught trespassing on federal property!" Tom shouted as he briefly blinded us with his bright flashlight.

We got up and quickly followed him through the tunnel, across the large room then up the stairs to outside. Night was turning into day, but the sun was still hiding. It slowly began to peek above the far-away Sierra range as we raced down the hill. I heard dogs barking. Thankfully, we made it safely to Tom's car.

As we drove away toward Marysville, I looked behind me as the sun's rays began to softly touch the ragged volcanic rocks on the high Buttes that the Maidu call Histum Yani (Spirit Mountain).

Many years later on a mid-winter trip to Gray Lodge Wildlife Sanctuary I gazed at the not-so-distant horizon where the Sutter Buttes stood, outlined by a gray and white painted sky. In the foreground a cacophony of migratory geese filled the chilly air.

As the sight took me back to my youthful escapades inside the long-abandoned missile silos, I was suddenly struck by the disconcerting contrast: the amazing intricacies of creation working seamlessly together, from the smallest organism to the vast universe, all guided by a benevolent hand, versus the current state of humankind with our bitter discord and military arsenals.

I offered up a short, silent prayer for world peace.

Chapter Nineteen

My Brother's Keeper

My brother Greg at Dunning Ave, Linda -
1959

My friends and I continued to visit the silos together but eventually I had to stop, since I was too busy with classes at Yuba College where I also had a part time job in the cafeteria. In addition, I was rebuilding a non-running old Chevy panel van that was the same year as my old pickup.

My second year at community college was ending and it was almost summer. When a classmate invited me to his house in Marysville for a party, I was excited and rather proud of myself, being from Linda, which was the wrong side of the Yuba River.

The party was in the backyard of a really nice place in Marysville. They had beautiful green lawns in the front yard as well as the back. That grass looked better than most carpets I'd ever seen. Plus, their outdoor furniture was real outdoor furniture and not some beat-up old couch or chair.

Holding my bottle of imported "Lowenbrau" beer, I hoped everyone would see the label and know that I was sophisticated. I had brought it specially for this occasion. But what no one else knew was that only the bottle was imported; I had saved some empties from Tony's restaurant where I used to work before it burned down and had filled some of those bottles with cheap beer from the grocery store.

Suddenly, someone yelled, "Fight!" So, I jogged over with the other looky-loos to see what was going on. That so-called fight consisted of the host of the party yelling at some teenager who was so drunk he could barely stand, let alone hold up his fists.

Trouble was, I'd known that kid most of my life and I knew his family. He was from my side of the river.

If that kid hadn't been so drunk, my moral obligation might have been simply to warn the other guy, since I knew what the kid was capable of. However, my conscience drove me to do something to save the kid from himself.

Putting my bottle of beer aside, along with my aspirations of upward social mobility, I ran up to the kid and pretended I was going to punch him. He flinched, and I dropped to my knee and lifted him onto my shoulder, thankful that I used to be a wrestler in high school.

I carried him down the street and around the corner to where I had hidden my rickety old pickup truck and threw him in the bed. Then I ran around to the cab and jumped in. I always left my keys in the ignition. Anyone who saw that truck would know why I never had to worry about someone stealing it. Besides, you had to use your foot to engage the starter and I figured most people wouldn't know that.

We took off out of Marysville across the Yuba River on that moonlit night and headed down Simpson Lane. There was commotion in the truck bed, and I could see in my rear-view mirror that the kid was trying to climb out of it while I was driving down the road. I jerked the steering wheel to make him fall back into the bed and had to keep doing that as we drove down Simpson Lane and onto Hammonton Road in Linda.

Suddenly I realized something. Man, if the cops see me driving like this, they're gonna think I'm drunk! Then I also realized I had those imported empties sitting on the floorboard. So, if I did get stopped for a suspected DUI, I could get cited for dangerous driving and having open containers.

Luckily, I made it to the end of a dirt road where I knew that kid lived. I stopped the truck, jumped out, ran around and opened the tailgate, then ran back into the cab. When he crawled out, and his feet hit the ground, I took off. As I was driving away, I looked into my mirror and saw the yellow front porch light turn on and watched our dad step outside.

Yep, that kid was my younger brother.

Now what am I going to do? I drove back to Marysville but was too embarrassed to go back to the party. Dammit Greg, you're always messing up my life.

Driving aimlessly around, I felt so bored I was hoping to get a flat tire just to have something to do. No one I knew was at Guys and Dolls Pool Hall or at any of the usual hangouts.

By the time I got back home, all the lights at our house were off. Grabbing a blanket and pillow from inside my trailer, I lay down outside on my cot and stared at the moon through the silhouette of a nearby oak tree.

God, I can't wait to leave this place. The thought of moving to Tahoe was more appealing than ever.

Days later, I briefly spoke to the college classmate who had invited me to his party.

"I heard that was your brother you carried away from my place. Is he okay?"

"Yeah, he's fine."

"That's good. By the way, I shared that bottle of Lowenbrau you left behind. Best beer we ever tasted." I bit my lip to stop from laughing.

Chapter Twenty

Leaving Linda

The primer brown vehicle sat alone in a weed-filled pasture near North Beale Road and Griffith Avenue when I spotted it.

"Is that your van?" I asked at a nearby house.

"It's my dad's," a teen-aged young man replied. "He's been planning to work on it, but he's sick."

"Can I look at it? I might want to buy it."

"Sure. Go ahead."

Through foxtails and star thistles, I strode toward the abandoned vehicle. All the tires were flat, and the back end sat at an odd angle. The passenger side rear-end leaf spring was bent. I lifted the heavy hood to check out the spiderweb-covered engine then closed it with a loud bang. *Looks like everything's there.*

The driver's side door made a spine-tingling screech when I cautiously opened it. A black widow fled below the worn-through bucket seat as I peered into the back. Someone had installed cabinets and a sleeping platform. Disintegrating flowery curtains fluttered in front of a partially opened small side window.

I walked behind the old truck and opened the door. A wasp's nest dropped to the ground and as I ran away, angry insects attacked me. Luckily, I only got stung twice. From a safe distance I looked through the open door.

It's a lot of work, but this'll be perfect.

After I offered the owner fifty dollars, we closed our deal, which included some spare parts. Then I needed to figure out how to get it towable enough to take home.

Mickey and I tried to pump up the van's tires but only two held air. Thankfully, the spare parts included two wheels with tires and an unbroken leaf spring. After much groaning, some words you never heard in the Bible, and copious sprays of WD-40, we had the leaf spring and tires replaced on "Ole Betsy" (her new nickname).

Backing my pickup to my project, we connected the two vehicles with a steel chain. I got back into my truck and watched in my rear-vision mirror as Mickey opened the van door and sat down in front of Ole Betsy's steering wheel. *Maybe I should have warned him about that black widow.* Slowly I drove forward to tighten the chain, then tried to inch forward but my truck stalled. I restarted it and tried again. Same result. Like an old person stuck in their ways, the primer brown panel truck wouldn't budge.

"I'll bet the parking brake's stuck," I told Mickey. "Hand me that WD-40 and I'll grab a hammer and crawl underneath."

I stomped down some weeds, squeezed myself between the van's underbody and the ground, then slid myself toward the parking brake mechanism. It was stuck. After a few sprays of WD-40 and a hard whack with my hammer, the brake pads released their grip on the driveshaft.

"Let's try again," I yelled. "She should move now."

And she did.

After driving through the field, I put my arm out the window and motioned for Mickey to stop. He slowly applied his brakes and we both stopped. It was good to have Mickey's help. He knew 'bout towin': "The towed vehicle does the stoppin'. That way, the chain stays taut."

I pulled onto Griffith for the short drive to North Beale Road. We waited, cautiously crossed, then continued to the dirt road which took us home, where we stopped under the huge limb of a poplar that would soon be my engine hoist.

Over a couple of months, I removed and rebuilt the engine, installed a new-to-me "four on the floor" transmission, replaced the hoses and fan belt, found a couple new-to-me bucket seats, cleaned up the interior and made some new curtains out of old blue jeans.

My plan was to live in the van while looking for work in the Lake Tahoe area. Eventually I wanted to attend the University of Nevada, Las Vegas to study Hotel and Restaurant Administration. However, to afford that, I'd have to become a Nevada State resident. In the meantime, I could work and go skiing.

Finally, Ole Betsy was ready to go, and so was I.

I sold my pickup and most of my meager belongings, making sure to keep my pressure cooker and skis. Early one morning in September 1974, I said goodbye to my family, drove to the end of our dirt road and turned left at Griffith Avenue. At Hammonton Road I turned *right* and drove east toward Tahoe. A short while after driving past Brophy School, I looked to the left and saw the rock piles of the Dredger Ponds. I thought of my pleasant times there and wondered if I'd ever be back. The rebuilt engine of my Chevy mobile home purred along, and I was proud of my accomplishment. Slowly, my van began to climb the foothills of the Sierra Nevada mountains.

Before reaching Highway 20 I pulled over and walked to a spot where I could look out over the Sacramento Valley. I could see Beale Air Force Base, the Olivehurst water tower and the small community where I grew up. I was leaving home. I was leaving Linda.

Chapter Twenty-One
Mining the Mind

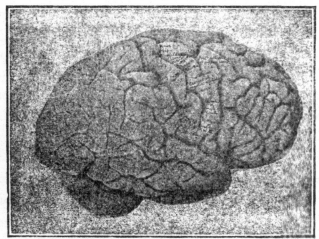

1907 image of a brain, from p. 39 "Labour and Childhood"
Margaret McMillan, Public domain, via Wikimedia Com-
mons

"Bullet, maybe you should become a monk," John, my Lake Tahoe roommate, told me one day. Bullet was the nickname my roommates gave me because they had a friend in LA called Bullet Bob.

"Why do you say that?"

"Well, you're not into partying. You don't gamble or chase women. You're a health food nut, contemplative and always studying something. Yep. You'd make a fine monk."

"I'll look into it," I said sarcastically as I headed off to work.

Hmm. I never really thought about that. How do you become a monk anyway? Go to monk school?

I was surprised John noticed my studying and thought I was contemplative. Maybe he saw some of the books I was reading for my Philosophy class at Lake Tahoe Community College. I took the class hoping to find some insights about life. However, that hope was crushed by my professor on the first day.

"Perhaps some of you are here to find answers about life. Unfortunately, at the end of this course, you'll probably be even more confused. Philosophy isn't necessarily about finding answers to life's perplexities. It's about mining of the mind. Or in other words, masturbating the mind."

Oh, that's clever and deep. I don't get it.

I never did figure out what he meant by that. It was just one more unanswered question, and I was afraid I might be wasting my time in his class. Still, I could learn *something* and get a few extra college credits.

Almost the same thing had happened when I took my first psychology class at Yuba College. The teacher said a lot of people study psychology to find out how to be happy.

"Unfortunately, people with psychology degrees aren't any happier than the general public. In fact, I'm willing to say, a lot of people in the mental health field have mental problems themselves."

As it turned out, I really enjoyed the psychology class and the instructor, a slightly built, perky woman, with short blond hair who was always challenging our assumptions. I still remember her saying, "When someone tells me they have an open mind, I usually discover the opposite." Among the books she had us read were *One Flew Over the Cuckoo's Nest* and *Brave New World,* by Aldous Huxley. Huxley's book inspired me to think more deeply and to question my belief system. Hopefully, my Tahoe philosophy class would do the same.

With the dream of eventually attending UNLV (University of Nevada, Las Vegas), I had moved in September of 1974 to South Lake Tahoe, California, near the Nevada border where I secured a Nevada post office box and did all my correspondence with the university using that as my mailing address to establish state residency.

After moving to Tahoe, my original plan was to stay in my '55 Chevy panel van.

I got a job at Sahara Tahoe Casino as a bus boy. An old acquaintance from Yuba College worked there and had told me the job included free meals, a place to shower, and tips. In about a week, I got tired of the meals, which were mostly leftover buffet food and learned the showers were only for chefs; but I did get tips every day.

I lived rent free in my van in the parking lot of the casino and showered at campgrounds. While sleeping in the parking lot, I was sometimes afraid I might witness a mugging, rape, or even a Mafia hit. After all, South Lake Tahoe was a big city compared to Linda. Luckily, nothing bad happened, although I was awakened one night by someone shouting, "Sit, Fifi. Now jump. Good girl. Rosy, sit, jump. Good girl." A dog trainer was practicing his act and I was able to watch for free.

The temperature dropped steeply in November. It started to snow lightly, and I didn't have a heater. In need of a better place to live I asked around at work.

Jack, another bus boy, said he and his buddy Skip were looking for someone.

I moved to the small three-bedroom house one day before a major snowstorm hit the region. I was grateful to re-enter civilization, and they were grateful for a new roommate, especially one that knew how to cook.

They were from Los Angeles and were surprised to learn I didn't know how to skate-board, had never surfed, had almost never driven on a freeway and grew up at the end of a dirt road.

Less than a month after my move, Jack announced he wanted to get a bigger, nicer house. Some of his city friends were interested in moving to Tahoe and needed a place to stay. Skip and I agreed with the idea and after we found a larger house, the LA onslaught began. Soon John, Scott, Rob, and David were at our door.

After that I was even more the odd man out, since all the guys were longtime buddies from LA, and I was the country bumpkin who got teased about my humble background. One evening, while several of us were watching the news on TV, the anchorman an-nounced,

We end this broadcast with a story out of Marysville. A small plane crashed into a cow on the runway at the Yuba County Airport. The cow and passengers reportedly are all doing fine, but the plane suffered considerable damage.

John was the first to make the connection.

"That's where you're from, right, Bullet?" he asked, chuckling.

"Uh, yeah."

"That's funny, a cow on the runway! What's next, a pig traffic jam on the Interstate?"

"Yuba County doesn't have an Interstate."

"Why doesn't that surprise me?" Dave chortled while the others hooted. John choked on his beer and almost fell off his chair.

I laughed along too. It was nice to have a good laugh, even at my hometown's expense.

Chapter Twenty-Two
Roommates

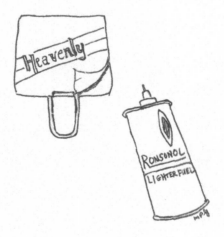

None of those new Tahoe roommates knew how to cook. They survived on meals from work, frozen convenience fare, and fast-food restaurants.

One advantage of being surrounded by cooking neophytes was my supplies were seldom stolen since they had to be cooked. A lot of it was also health food.

You never heard me cry out, "Who the hell stole my tofu again?" Or brewer's yeast, bean sprouts, brown rice, dried beans, or homemade yogurt.

Jack, my original roommate, often took up a collection to "buy" food for me to prepare. Since I was the cook, I didn't have to contribute. I'd give him a list of ingredients and later learned he would shoplift the items and pocket the money.

He also had a scheme to go skiing for free. He'd visit resorts in the afternoon and as people were finishing for the day, ask if he could have their lift ticket. The tickets came with a peel-off backing and a stiff wire. After you peeled off the back, the ticket folded over against itself and around the wire, which then looped through your zipper pull tab. Jack would clip the ticket off the person's jacket with wire cutters then go to his car and coat it with lighter fluid to separate it. He'd then grab a new wire and reattach the ticket to his own jacket zipper.

One of Jack's other cons was to get free meals at the buffet where we worked. Buffet customers who wanted to use the restroom had to leave the room and of course walk past numerous gambling enticements. To reenter the buffet, they had to show a receipt. Jack would somehow alter receipts he or a friend gathered from trash cans while working and use them to gain buffet entry for himself and usually a friend. His con was discovered after he re-used a *dinner for six* receipt to provide free meals for five friends, most of whom were our mutual housemates.

(Fortunately, I had night classes, otherwise I might have been included in Jack's dinner scam.) A suspicious hostess caught them and all except David, who worked as a carpenter for a building contractor, were fired from their casino jobs, even if they were working at a different casino.

When Jack couldn't find work, he moved back to LA and got into politics. Actually, I don't know what Jack did after leaving Tahoe, but politics might have suited him.

One evening in mid-December I was working late updating the menu board for the buffet and the manager walked up to me.

"Bob. You might want to make plans to go home for Christmas. I scheduled you off for the holidays. By the way, you're the only one getting off."

"Why me? I didn't even ask."

"That's why. You're the only person that didn't ask. You might want to keep it a secret, everyone will be jealous."

As I added *Christmas Buffet!* to the menu board I contemplated hitch- hiking home instead of driving. It would be another adventure. But what would I do with the frozen turkey we were getting for a bonus? Maybe I could carry it in my backpack and cook it for Christmas dinner. That would be my gift to the family.

A couple of days before Christmas I was standing on the roadside hitching a ride toward Truckee. A police officer drove by. Good thing I was on the California side of the border and not in Nevada where hitchhiking is illegal.

I chuckled at the thought of getting interrogated.

"What's in the backpack?"

"Turkey."

"What'd you call me?"

"No, no, no. There's a frozen turkey in my backpack. I'm bringing it home for my impoverished family for Christmas dinner. Last year all they could afford was Banquet Turkey Pot Pies. Please don't arrest me, officer!"

While I was amusing myself with imaginary conversations, a pickup pulled over and a young man gave me a ride to Truckee. He dropped me off at an I-80 on-ramp and as I sat on a guardrail, I realized something: my dad probably set the grade for this ramp when the freeway was being built.

I hadn't even stuck out my thumb when a light blue Cadillac pulled over and a female voice cried out from the passenger window.

"Need a ride?"

Wow. Must be the Christmas spirit.

"Yep, I'm headin' to Marysville."

"It's your lucky day, we're going to Chico."

As I walked closer to the fancy car, I heard the latch to the trunk click. The driver, a middle-aged, clean-shaven man, got out and opened the trunk further. He moved a suitcase.

"Put your pack right there."

Whew. I'd have been kind of nervous sitting next to a defrosting turkey inside a warm car.

Soon we merged onto I-80. Inside the nicest vehicle I had ever ridden in, I marveled at the snow-covered mountains and breathtaking scenery, imagining how difficult it must have been for workers, including my dad, to build the freeway I was riding on. As we began climbing toward Donner Summit, I saw snow sheds clinging to the mountainside, built to protect the train track from excess snow.

I never imagined that many years later I'd hike through those tunnels with my two grown sons.

My chauffeur turned on the radio after he'd left the freeway and drove toward Marysville on Hwy 20. Christmas music played.

This was nice. I kind of felt like royalty and was sure glad I'd decided to hitchhike.

"I can drop you off at your home in Marysville. Where is it?" my driver asked as we drove through Penn Valley.

"It's actually in Linda. If you don't mind, you can take Hammonton-Smartsville into Marysville. It wouldn't be too far out of your way."

"Don't mind at all. Know the area well."

Soon we were driving into the Sacramento Valley and past the dredger ponds.

"Turn left here," I said as we approached Griffith Ave. "Just let me off in front of that dirt road," I continued seconds later.

"You sure? I can give you a ride to the end."

"It's pretty rough. I'd feel better if you didn't. Just pop open the trunk and I'll grab my pack. Thanks so much for the ride. Merry Christmas!"

Walking toward home, I navigated around a few small potholes. When I got to the large puddle where you'd usually have to shimmy around the corner against the fence, I just walked through it. With the added weight in my backpack, I wasn't about to risk losing my balance. Luckily, I had on my rubber-bottomed snow boots.

My Christmas dinner was a success. We had mashed potatoes, gravy, and roasted vegetables along with the twenty-pound bird. After spending a couple of relaxing days with the family, I took a bus back to Tahoe.

Decades later my dad would still enjoy reminiscing about "that time Bobby hitch-hiked home from Tahoe, with a frozen turkey on his back." My wife and kids would hear it re-told many times.

Chapter Twenty-Three
Or Stupid

Parasailing - Public domain - Lake Tahoe Visitors Authority Image

Back in Tahoe in late Spring, a coworker of one of my roommates, after witnessing parasailing in Acapulco, had an idea to start a parasailing business, since the activity wasn't yet popular in the US. He had purchased a parasail and asked at a party, "Who wants to be the first person to try it out?"

"I'll do it. Sounds like fun."

Several days later I was strapped in a harness as several of my so-called friends held onto the parasail behind me. Unfortunately, the rope that was connected to my harness wasn't connected to a speed boat in the clear pure waters of Lake Tahoe. Instead, it was tied to the bumper of a pickup truck sitting on a dirt road in an open field littered with trash.

"Okay, I'll take the slack out of the rope as I slowly drive forward. Then I'll speed up and everyone run behind me," shouted Kirk, driver and owner of the parasail.

Once the rope tightened, the parasail began to fill with air and my friends let go. Within seconds I was airborne. I was flying!... For about ten seconds, with my feet about a foot off the ground. Our first parasail experiment might have been a success if it wasn't for that blasted manual transmission. When Kirk shifted into second gear the rope sagged and I dropped to the ground. I couldn't run as fast as the truck, so I was dragged along the ground. I could see a busted beer bottle ahead that would have inflicted serious damage on me if the truck didn't stop. Luckily, it did stop only inches before I reached the broken glass.

Kirk ran from the truck.

"You all right, Bullet?"

"Yeah, I'm fine. That was fun while it lasted."

"I'm going to have to rent a boat after all. Who wants to try this on the lake?"

The others shook their heads vigorously.

"Heck, I'll do it again." I stood up and started to brush myself off. "Should be a lot safer than this. Boats don't have manual transmissions, do they?"

This is much better...a beautiful sunny day...a bit windy though...a powerful speed boat docked in front of me, ready to take me for a parasail ride above a pristine lake, while curious onlookers snap photos of this daring young man as I stand on the beach strapped in my harness... What could go wrong?

Someone said, "I heard this is the first time they've ever tried this. That guy must be brave!"

Or stupid.

The boat engine roared as Paul revved the motor. I knew the routine. It was like water skiing except I was on land, and I'd be running towards the water. The ground crew, David and John, held onto the parasail as Paul motored slowly forward and took the slack out of the rope. Then he gunned it. I barely took a step forward as the parasail quickly filled with air and I was suddenly airborne.

Paul turned right toward Nevada and showed me a bird's eye view of the South Lake Tahoe shoreline. People along the shore were staring, including a photographer from the *Tahoe Tribune* who took my picture for the paper.

Minutes later, Paul began to reverse course to bring me back. As he made a U-turn the parasail was running with the wind. It started descending and it looked like I would be taking a dunk. With my feet only inches from the water, we finally made the turn and headed back. Once we picked up speed, I sailed higher and higher. As we turned toward the shore, I worried there wasn't much room for me to put down.

We should have used a bigger beach.

I had little control over where I'd alight. It was mostly up to Paul.

My God...what if I land in the trees? Or in the busy street? Or hit a car in the parking lot?

The boat stopped near the shoreline. I didn't. The wind carried me over the crowd on the beach and they scattered. I barely avoided hitting a sign stating the rules concerning beach use (which didn't mention anything about parasailing) then safely landed standing up as a small crowd cheered.

We wisely moved our operation to a bigger beach with fewer obstacles. Other friends were now willing to take up the challenge and it all went smoothly, except when David landed in a small tree. Paul, who was heavy, took a turn at parasailing but hit the water when the boat, unable to cope with his weight, lost speed while trying to return to the shore.

Paul, the pioneer, gave up his plans to start a parasailing business in Lake Tahoe. Word was he couldn't afford the insurance premiums. He opened a sandwich shop in Berkeley instead.

Chapter Twenty-Four
Bar Boy Bob

Since I was working and going to school, I spent little time at home. There was always someone new moving in or out. I kept out of the roommate disputes, paid my rent and with Jack gone, no one took up a collection to buy food for me to cook.

To expand my knowledge of the hotel-restaurant business, I decided to try for a job at Harrah's Casino as an apprentice bartender, AKA, Bar Boy. I obtained an interview and before the meeting, got a haircut.

"We usually don't hire people that are only twenty-two as Bar Boys. We want people that are interested in making this their career. But we'll give you a chance. You'll have to get a haircut before you start though," said the beverage supervisor.

After getting another haircut and working for a few days, the shift supervisor took me aside, "Bob, your hair's too long. You need to get a haircut." So, three haircuts in one week. Must be a record.

The job as Bar Boy was quite challenging. You had to keep the bars stocked with liquor, beer, ice, glasses, lemons, limes, and whatever was needed. One of the toughest bars to work was a circular bar we nicknamed "The Racetrack" because you'd spend your whole shift running around in a circle. It was so busy, you seldom had time for a pit stop.

At that time, to become a bartender at Harrah's, you had to attend their Bar School. To get into that you had to first become a Bar Boy and be voted in by the bartenders. Some guys had been trying for over five years to become bartenders.

"You'd better make sure you keep my bar fully stocked or I won't vote for you to get into Bar School," a gruff-looking man in his late forties grumbled to me one evening. The threat fell on deaf ears. I was about as interested in making bartending my life's work as I was in becoming a Go-Go Dancer.

To get a break from the noise and smoke of the casino floor, I volunteered for jobs that most Bar Boys weren't interested in because the tips weren't good. One of those jobs was the fancy restaurant at the top of Harrah's. The pace of the restaurant was slower and served a different clientele. Also, when the Bar School-trained bartender left for lunch or a break, it was okay for the lowly Bar Boy to mix drinks.

Another place a Bar Boy could mix drinks was the showroom, since it was so busy. I was pretty much left alone getting everything ready before customers started entering. Then the action began!

About a dozen or so bartenders and Bar Boys mixed hundreds of drinks before the show started. Once the last drink was served it was "quiet time." Noises from the kitchen were not allowed. My job was now to stand in the background and be at the ready in case I was needed to serve late-comers, get something for the performers, or take care of minor emergencies.

While standing in the background near a curtain that separated the showroom from the kitchen, I got to see Don Rickles, Sammy Davis Jr., The Lawrence Welk Show, Wayne Newton and others. At first, watching the shows for free was exciting. However, hearing Newton sing *Daddy Don't You Walk So Fast* for three weeks in a row got boring. It was especially irritating to have the song stuck in my head and to hear Newton say at *every* performance, "You're the best audience I've had all week!"

If I was wearing my Bar Boy jacket, security knew it was okay for me to be standing there. Occasionally, various Bar Boys would stop by during their breaks and switch places with me so they could watch the shows.

"Bullet Bob. I heard I'd find you here," cried the familiar voice as I was preparing for Sammy Davis Jr's upcoming show. It was Jack!

"How'd you get past security? Never mind. I don't want to know. What brings you back to Tahoe?"

"I'm here to do some skiing and visit old friends. I heard you get to watch shows for free. You think I could borrow your jacket when the show starts?"

I should have known that was why he came to see me.

"What! I could get fired for doing that. You already caused several people to lose their jobs. But all right, I'm planning to quit this job soon anyway. Come back when the show starts, reach through the curtain and tap me on the shoulder. I'll give you my jacket then. You can wear it for fifteen minutes."

As expected, not long after the show started there was a tap on my shoulder.

"I'll be standing right behind you," I whispered after going behind the curtain and handing Jack my jacket.

Several minutes later a cocktail waitress approached Jack.

"Where's Bob?"

"Right here, Amanda. What can I get for you?" I murmured as I peeked out from behind the curtain.

She looked at Jack, then me. She knew what was going on and made a wry smile.

"Some old bag says her sloe gin fizz isn't fizzy enough."

"Probably 'cuz it isn't. I'll make a new one," I replied in a stage whisper. Those drinks sat for quite some time before they were served. I was surprised we didn't get more complaints.

After mixing the drink, I tapped Jack on the shoulder, and he came through the curtain.

"Give this to Amanda please. You've got about seven minutes of jacket use left."

After his seven minutes were up, I tapped Jack on the shoulder again. He wouldn't leave! I continued to poke and prod him, but he wouldn't budge. About five minutes later he finally joined me behind the curtain and gave me back my jacket.

I wanted to strangle him, but it would've made too much noise.

Chapter Twenty-Five
Purpose

When I visited Lake Tahoe Community College, I found that since it was the college's first year, classes were to take place in a converted motel. The motel rooms had been transformed into classrooms which were well-lit and freshly painted. A board member once proudly proclaimed to the local press that they were the college with the most bathrooms per student.

I enrolled in a journalism course, helped produce the student newspaper and wrote a few articles. The paper created some controversy when a story about a blind student was published. The reporter asked the student what it would be like to see again.

"If I woke up tomorrow morning and could see my sock, I'd be excited," was the reply.

Because of a possibly intentional typo, the quote in the paper read, "If I woke up tomorrow morning and could see my cock, I'd be excited."

Our Journalism instructor told us some people wanted to discontinue the newspaper because of the hullabaloo.

Luckily, the school administration allowed us to continue distributing the paper, which wasn't too surprising since the school's president was also the Philosophy professor who spoke about "masturbating the mind".

Many of the journalism students were colorful personalities and well educated. Some had university degrees and simply liked publishing a newspaper. Jake, from New Orleans, hosted a pre-Mardi Gras party in the early spring. The party was interesting, and I even brought a date who was a waitress from work. She was cute and nice, but we didn't have much in common and I was too shy to carry on a decent conversation.

Another student got the address wrong and while dressed as a scuba diver, complete with flippers, waddled up to the wrong address. No one answered the door, so he walked to the side of the house to peek into a window. He soon discovered that flippers do not work well in the snow, fell backward, and could not get back up. A neighbor heard the commotion, and when he saw the strange creature in the yard, called the police. They arrived and helped him up. Surprisingly, they believed his story of searching for a pre-Mardi Gras celebration and after a good laugh let him go. Sadly, he never found the party.

I thought it would be interesting to take an Early Childhood Education class. I was the only male in a class of over twenty students. One day our class visited a day care center. Two children came up to me separately and asked, "Are you my daddy?" which became a sad memory.

Harrah's was giving me more hours than I wanted. Summer was approaching and I knew it was going to get even busier. One day I worked an exhausting thirteen-hour shift and as I left the casino, the sun was rising. A few days later I gave my two weeks' notice. My supervisors were upset. I guess they were right: they shouldn't have hired a twenty-two-year-old.

It was time to leave Tahoe and begin my studies at the University of Nevada, Las Vegas. However, before moving to Vegas, I needed a vacation. My sister and I borrowed our mother's VW station wagon and drove to Northern Minnesota to spend time with the One-Eyed Banker from Bigfork, our grandfather.

Accompanying us was Larry, a friend I made in Tahoe who was heading back to Peoria, his hometown.

He had joined me in parasailing, hitchhiking to Yosemite for a backpacking trip, and other adventures.

We enjoyed our drive through America's countryside, camping along the way in campgrounds and Yellowstone National Park. Eventually we reached Minnesota and a dirt road near our grandfather's cabin, which was about a fifteen-minute drive from Bigfork. Suddenly a bear ran across our path.

"Wow, a bear!" exclaimed Larry. "That's a cool omen. Bears represent the courage to evolve and the ability to be open-minded."

"So, it's a good sign?" Karen asked.

"Sure," I responded, "unless it's a grizzly and it's running after you."

When we got to the cabin and told Grandpa, he said, "Really? I haven't seen a bear in years."

The next day, I drove Larry to Grand Rapids to catch a Greyhound bus home.

It was a relief getting away from the hustle and bustle of Lake Tahoe. We visited relatives, went fishing, canoeing, water skiing and enjoyed the tranquil life, until one day...

"*Help! Slim* (my grandfather's nickname)! *Help!*"

We had just sat down for lunch at the cabin, which was next to Horseshoe Lake. Hurrying outside, we could see a capsized boat with several people in the water about a quarter of a mile away.

"It's Ed and Thelma and their friends. Karen, call the police! Bobby, jump onto the pontoon boat with me!"

We sped toward the accident where four elderly people were in the water. One man was safely clinging to the capsized boat. Grandpa pulled his boat next to Ed who was drowning and grabbed him. I dove into the water and brought Thelma and her friend to the nearby shoreline.

"Bobby! I can't help him! He's not breathing and he's too heavy for me to get him onto the boat!"

I swam over to Ed, who was overweight, and struggled to bring him to the shoreline but finally made it. I then performed mouth-to-mouth resuscitation. Thankfully, he started breathing. Thelma was ecstatic.

"You saved his life! Thank God! Thank God!"

I could hear sirens and soon the sheriff and an ambulance arrived. Once Ed was heading to the hospital, the sheriff had a few words to say to the reckless boaters.

"You folks are sure lucky. If it weren't for Slim and this young man here, at least one of you would be dead. Your boat was overloaded, and you weren't wearing life jackets. This could have easily happened somewhere on the lake where no one would have heard you."

Back at the cabin as I sat down to finish lunch, I realized my glasses were missing. I had failed to remove them before diving into the lake.

"Don't worry," Grandpa commented, his good eye twinkling. "I'm sure Ed and Thelma will buy you a new pair."

"Maybe so. But I'd like to find them. After lunch I'll go snorkeling."

After many attempts over two days, I found my glasses stuck in the mud at the bottom of the lake.

Saving those people was uplifting. It meant I had value. Because of me, they were alive.

I had visited Minnesota a year earlier with the original plan to visit my grandparents for their fiftieth wedding anniversary. Sadly, my grandmother died before the celebration. I chose to go to Minnesota anyway because my grandfather didn't drive, seldom cooked and could use some help.

During that time, I drove my grandfather around and became his personal chef. He even invited some of his friends over to experience my cooking. I also spent a lot of time reading. I had brought books on philosophy, spiritually inclined books, and Thoreau's *Walden*. I could especially relate with Thoreau when I was living in a cabin by a lake. Horseshoe Lake was my Walden Pond.

In my grandfather's library at his apartment in Bigfork I discovered an obscure book, *The Book of Unlearning*. The book pointed out many of the contradictions in the Bible and promoted a new type of religion based upon truths from other faiths and unity between science and religion. I was intrigued and wondered whose book it might have been. My mother's? Uncle Bob's? Maybe even my grandparents', which I doubted since they were devout Lutherans. I never did find out.

Along with my reading, an inner voice was calling me to a higher purpose: to help others. To make a difference in the world that would add value to my life. But what would I do?

C. F. Gilbertson - "Slim"

Chapter Twenty-Six
Smelling Pinecones

The sun it sets so silently
Waves roll in at my feet
I gaze upon a distant star
And wonder who we are
"Brave men are we,"
I've heard them say
But can you kiss a flower,
Or a child?
-Bob Gauper, age 23

The sun set as I stood at the Pacific Ocean and breathed the salty air. Waves crashed nearby then gently released their awesome power at my bare feet. I could hear the murmur of my cousin Joey and sister Karen chatting next to a small fire. Karen sat a little awkwardly, one leg still in a cast from her water-skiing mishap in Minnesota.

We had left Minnesota a week earlier. Joey, a professional bartender in his early twenties, had never been away from the Midwest until he decided to join us on our adventure back to California.

Joey grew up in the northern Minnesota mining and papermill town of Grand Rapids. Dark-haired and good-looking, he had an active social life that included heavy drinking. Usually he lived with his mother, who worked as a baker at the Piggly Wiggly, where she was known as Pasty Queen of the Iron Range; her husband, Joey's dad, had left the family when Joey was a boy.

Joey had a large scar across his chest where he had lassoed a frying pan of hot bacon and pulled it off the stove while playing cowboy as a kid. You could still see the beginning of the scar just above his collar line. His only sibling, an older sister, lived in Alaska.

We were taking the long way home, driving along Hwy 2 across Minnesota, North Dakota, and Montana. Along the way, we stayed in campgrounds with Karen sleeping in the cream-colored station wagon and Joey and me in a small tent. In Montana, we visited Glacier National Park and hoped to camp there, but all the facilities were fully booked. While exploring one of those crowded campgrounds, I noticed the strangest thing: someone watching television inside a tent.

"That's weird. Watching TV, while in one of the most beautiful places in America?"

"I dunno, seems kinda neat. What's on?" Joey asked.

"I wouldn't know, I never watch TV." Joey and I were so different, it continually amazed me.

Joey and I took turns driving west through the night. I worried that somehow, we should have spent more time at Glacier. We were supposed to be on vacation, but this wasn't relaxing. *Go here. Go there. See this, see that.* We weren't taking time to smell the pinecones. Then something happened that completely altered the pace and atmosphere of our journey. It was after we arrived in Crescent City, California.

"Shoot!" I exclaimed when the Volkswagen wouldn't move after I started it.

"What's wrong?" Karen asked.

"There's something wrong with the clutch."

Opening the panel to look at the engine while Joey pushed in the clutch, I didn't notice anything I could fix. In any case, I had no tools.

It was the weekend, and no repair shop was open, so we camped out near the beach, which turned out to be the best experience of our westward journey, at least for me. Now I *had* to slow down. Sleeping in the tent while listening to ocean waves, walking along the beach and writing a poem about it, had the effect of calming my uneasy spirit. *I'm going to be more spontaneous when I go on an adventure again,* I told myself.

Monday, I had the car towed and the shop staff said it would take at least a week to get the needed part. Studying the map, I pondered our situation. *Over three hundred miles back to Marysville. Maybe we could make it home without a clutch.*

Stopping to smell pinecones or write poems about ocean waves would be nice, but I had to get to Las Vegas soon. As captain of the Volkswagen ship, I had to trust my instincts, even if no one else would. Driving without a clutch it would be.

Chapter Twenty-Seven
Running Stop Signs

"**W**hatcha thinkin'?" my sister asked.

"I'm thinkin' we try to make it home. I change gears all the time in my panel van without using the clutch. But that's when it's already running. If we can start the Volkswagen while it's in gear my idea might work. Every time we stop, I'll have to turn off the car and we'll have to restart it. Let's give it a try. What have we got to lose?"

"Um... our lives?" Joey's voice cracked.

I paid the tow bill and told the shop owner my plan.

"Sounds feasible if you can start the car. I'd think about doin' that for a few miles. But Marysville? That's a long way. Good luck."

∞

"I'll sit inside and engage the starter while both of you push. If it starts, you'll have to run and jump in."

"Um...running and jumping? My leg's in a cast, y'know," Karen protested.

"Oh yeah...Let's give it a try though. If we can't get the VW going, we'll have to figure something else out."

"Okay...hope I don't trip and break my other leg."

"Push!" I shouted while turning the ignition key. The vehicle moved forward a few feet then started! Joey ran and jumped inside. Karen hobbled behind as I slowed down as much as possible. She made it!

I circled the small parking lot and waved at the shop owner and a mechanic who waved back while shaking their heads.

Thankfully, the road was free of cars, and I pulled onto the street without stopping. About half a mile away, I ran my first stop sign.

"I'll be running a lot of these. Hey Karen, how 'bout you keep track?"

In the distance I saw a red traffic light, drove into a shopping center parking lot and circled around until the light turned green, then drove back into the street.

Soon we were going south on highway 101 towards 299 where we would head east. The hour and a half drive toward McKinleyville went well and soon we were traveling on 299 toward Redding. The winding, roller-coaster-like mountain road had me doubting my decision to drive home. Our most harrowing experience was when the car stalled behind a slow-moving gravel truck laboring its way up a steep grade. Miraculously, I quickly made a U-turn and coasted down the mountain to find a place to pull over.

"This is crazy," Joey finally exhaled after I had stopped.

"Maybe so. But what else can we do? Let's have some lunch and wait to see if any big trucks pass. If we're not behind any, we shouldn't have a problem."

No trucks passed as we ate our cold sandwiches, and soon I was driving back through the mountains toward home. We safely made it to Weaverville and stopped for gas. I looked at the map.

"We're already two-thirds of the way toward Redding. Before long we'll be heading south on I-5," I reassured my passengers.

"That'll be a welcome sight. No stop lights or stop signs. No mountains," my sister sighed.

It *was* a welcome sight when we finally made it to the freeway. I was confident we'd make it home safely now. In about an hour, we'd leave the freeway near Willows and take the back roads home. In close to eight hours and 114 missed stop signs since leaving Crescent City, we watched the sun set as I drove down the dirt road, between tall rows of corn, toward our house. An old Labrador and an excited cross-eyed Chihuahua with bad teeth ran to greet us. Finally, we were back home in Linda, at least for a short while. It was now time to get ready for my big move to Vegas.

Chapter Twenty-Eight
Ramblin' and Gamblin'

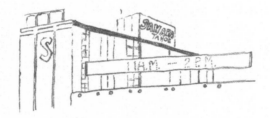

Dad had one of his shade tree mechanic friends fix the Volkswagen. I wished I had time to work on it, but it was already August and my first semester at UNLV was starting soon. Plus, Joey was getting anxious. He wasn't impressed with the Sacramento Valley in late summer. It was way too hot, flat, and he missed his friends and girlfriend back in Grand Rapids.

"How soon we leavin'?" he kept asking.

"Soon as I finish tuning up my van. You don't want us breaking down, do you? It's a long way to Vegas, 'specially by way of Tahoe. I called my friend John, and he said we can spend the night at his place."

Early next morning, Dad made us breakfast and we said goodbye to my family. *Ole Betsy*, my primer brown panel van was ready for the journey.

As I ascended the Sierra mountains through Placerville toward South Lake Tahoe, I was extremely appreciative to have a working clutch.

When we arrived in South Lake Tahoe around noon, I showed Joey the converted motel community college where I used to go to school, the beach where I risked my life parasailing and the Sahara Casino parking lot where I used to stay.

"Wanna try our luck at the tables?" asked Joey.

"Nah, I don't gamble."

"Whaddaya mean you don't gamble? Drivin' hundreds of miles without a clutch?" Joey laughed, incredulous. "And being a parasailing guinea pig? At least I only play with money, not my life!"

Joey was right. Even my planned move to Vegas was a bit of a gamble. I was quite nervous about UNLV and unsure of myself but didn't want to admit that to him. I just shrugged.

"Yeah, you've got a point. Anyway, you can try your luck here at the Sahara. My friend Rob works here as beverage supervisor and might even offer you a job."

We walked into the casino and stood by the buffet where I used to work. A young woman was changing the words on the sign near the buffet entrance.

"You go waste your money and I'll see if I can find Rob," I told Joey.

He strolled toward a Blackjack table.

"I used to do that years ago," I said to the girl as she closed the glass door on the sign.

"Bet you're glad you don't do it anymore."

"Yep. It wasn't so bad, though, I was glad to have a job in Tahoe."

My route to the beverage office took me past the employee dining room and I was happy I no longer ate there. Burgers. Fries. Leftover buffet food. Now that I was trying to be a vegetarian, none of that food appealed to me.

"Hey Bob!" a voice called out from an open office door. It was Tom, my former classmate from Yuba College.

"What're you up to? Looking to get your old job back?"

"Nah. On my way to Vegas to attend UNLV. Stopping by to see old friends. Is Rob around? He used to be my roommate."

"He took today off. Said an old friend is coming to visit. That must be you."

"Have a safe trip. Good luck."

"Thanks Tom. Nice to see you," I said as I departed his office.

Joey had left the blackjack table. I found him sitting at a bar chatting with a nice-looking blonde.

"Rob's off today. He's probably home waiting for us. Let's go."

He took the last swallow of his drink and said goodbye to the lady.

We met Rob and my other friends at their house. We talked and laughed about old times. Later they treated Joey and me to dinner at a nightclub. The waitress knew Rob and John since they were regulars. When I ordered a bottle of Perrier water, John quipped, "Yep, Bullet, I still think you should look into becoming a monk."

While we ate, a band played background music. After a song finished, I saw the singer staring at our table then Rob nodding.

"This next song is dedicated to Bullet."

Rob slowly took a swig from a bottle of Budweiser as the song began.

Las Vegas ain't no place for a poor boy like me...

John was laughing quietly. I was shocked and amused; I'd never had a song dedicated to me before. They must have planned this when they knew I was coming.

"Gee thanks, guys," I said as the song ended. After eating, my table mates continued drinking and began dancing when a new band playing disco music came out. I went outside for some fresh air.

Suddenly I felt even more anxious about my move. Could it be my friends knew me better than I knew myself?

Vegas is the best place to advance my education in the hotel and restaurant industry. But it's all so shallow. Casinos. Drinking and gambling. Fast women. Maybe Las Vegas isn't the place for me. Maybe I should become a monk.

But this was no time to give up. My tuition was all paid and we were set to leave the next day.

Chapter Twenty-Nine
Alone in Sin City

On our way out of town in the early evening, "Ole Betsy" took Joey and me past Lake Tahoe Community College, the Red Hut Waffle Shop where I'd sometimes meet friends for breakfast, then near the house where I first lived with Jack and Skip. We drove between El Dorado Beach, my parasailing beach, and the campground across the street where I used to sneak in to take showers. We continued traveling near the lake's shoreline to the

Sahara Casino at the border of California and Nevada. I reminisced about when I first pulled into that parking lot looking for a job with only a hundred dollars in my pocket. In a couple more minutes at Hwy 207, I turned right to head east and pointed to the post office as we drove by.

"I only got junk mail and letters from the university. Still can't believe I got Nevada residency."

"Hope all that scheming works out for you," replied Joey.

Looking in the mirror as we traveled along Kingsbury Grade Highway, I could see the lake behind me. My years in Tahoe had been good to me. I'd made new friends, attended college, and had many new and exciting experiences. Soon we were winding our way down the steep grade out of the Sierras into Nevada's vast Carson Valley. Roadside business signs beckoned us to Carson City. Never would I have imagined that in the distant future I'd have two daughters who'd end up living there.

We continued onward as the eastern side of the moisture-blocking Sierra-Nevada Mountains towered nearby. As we passed irrigated pastures, I tried to recognize where I had once spent the night sleeping in an open field.

"A couple of years ago," I told Joey, "My friend Larry and I spent all day trying to hitchhike out of Yosemite without any luck. We had to sleep in the forest. Finally, the next morning, this guy in a beat-up station wagon stopped. We were grateful for the ride 'til we found out the driver, Sam, was an ex-con that just got out of prison and the brakes on his old Plymouth only worked when he pumped them. He also already had a passenger that might have been a teen-age runaway. Kid didn't even have a pair of shoes or a shirt. Driving down Tioga Pass without decent brakes was horrifying."

"Even scarier than driving through the mountains without a clutch?"

"Yup. I later found out that road has the steepest elevation drop in California. When Sam stopped for gas, he hit us up for gas money, and bought a fifth of Jack Daniels as well."

"Oh, to sip along the way. Did he share?"

"Heck no... so anyway, he was heading to Carson City, but *insisted* he could give us a ride all the way to South Lake Tahoe if we had somewhere they could stay overnight. We lied and said we wanted to spend more time exploring Nevada. Somewhere near Gardnerville Sam dropped us off. We spent the night sleeping in a pasture and woke up to a bunch of mooing cows staring at us."

"Dang Bobby, you're so crazy," Joey exhaled, stretching his long arms above the passenger seat.

The sun had almost set after we drove through Yerington then headed south on Hwy 95. There was no traffic and I marveled at the emptiness of Nevada as we continued toward Vegas. In a short while, we stopped at Walker Lake and there was still enough light to see the barren shoreline.

"Sure looks different than Minnesota lakes. I wonder why there's hardly any vegetation. Looks kind of creepy...how 'bout you drive now? I'll try sleeping in the back."

"Okay."

Although the road was mostly straight and flat, Joey kept weaving the van in a slight zig-zag motion as we headed south. His driving lasted about ten minutes.

"The steering's too sloppy. How do you drive this thing?"

"Guess it takes a special touch. She's like an old horse. Treat her right and she'll treat you right. Just pull over, I'll drive."

He obliged and I took the reins. After about an hour, I turned off onto a dirt road and stopped; grabbed my sleeping bag and pad, climbed to the top of the van and lay down. The quiet, star-filled night amazed me. A shooting star shot across the sky. It was so peaceful. The only sound I could hear was the contracting metal of Ole Betsy cooling down as she also took a well-deserved rest. After a nap of over an hour, we continued along the highway. At Tonopah, I stopped for gas and a cup of coffee as Joey stayed sleeping.

I stopped again a little later to relieve myself of my cup of coffee, then continued onward. Occasionally, a lone car would pass by us. As we approached Vegas, in the early morning hours, the sky ahead shone like a gigantic light bulb, such a contrast to the darkness of the desert.

"Hey Joey. Time to wake up. We're coming into the big city."

Weary-eyed, he climbed forward into the passenger seat. As we approached the metropolis, I was surprised the traffic was so heavy at four in the morning.

"Drive carefully. These people might be drunk."

"I dunno. Maybe closer to the strip, but a lot of people might be driving to or from work."

"Speakin' of the strip, let's go there. I'd like some breakfast."

"Okay. Grab the map and tell me how to get there."

I thought of *The Beverly Hillbillies* television show as we drove onto the strip. Ole Betsy looked so out of place amongst the limos and fancy cars, I hoped she wasn't embarrassed.

I started humming the show's theme song. Joey pointed at a garish sign: *Steak & Eggs - $2.99.*

"Stop! That's what I want."

I parked and Joey got out while I climbed in back and immediately fell asleep. Hours later, Joey was back, and he didn't look good.

"The steak and eggs were a waste of money. Meat was tough and the eggs were greasy. Plus, speaking of money, I kept losing at the blackjack tables. I'd better buy a bus ticket home before I'm broke. Someone told me there's a Greyhound station within walking distance."

"You sure?"

"Yeah, I'm sure. Looks like Las Vegas ain't no place for a poor boy like *me*."

He left to find the bus station while I took some fruit and yogurt out of the ice chest for breakfast. In a short while, Joey was back.

"The bus leaves to St. Louis tomorrow morning and there I transfer to Minneapolis. Then it's onto Grand Rapids.

"Did you know Greyhound started in Hibbing by giving rides to miners?"

"Yeah, I did. My dad told me about that."

"So, what now?" asked Joey. "Could we walk around the strip? You're moving here, but I'm leaving tomorrow. Might never be here again."

We walked around the strip and in and out of casinos for a couple of hours. Joey was mesmerized. As for me, if I'd seen one, I'd seen them all. The same scantily clad cocktail waitresses, noisy slot machines, gambling tables, and smoke-filled rooms. They gave me a headache. We returned to the van, and I drove toward Lake Mead.

We found a campsite near the lake where Joey slept in his small tent while I slept in the van. Early next morning I dropped him off outside the Greyhound station where we shook hands and said our goodbyes. He turned and walked away, carrying a small suitcase.

Joey was the only cousin I ever got to know well. Although his character was different from mine, I'd miss him. He did come back to the West and became a professional bartender in Tahoe, but it would be over ten years before I'd see him again. As he entered the bus station, I realized the only person I knew in Vegas was leaving. I was alone in Sin City.

Chapter Thirty
Vegas Vignettes

Las Vegas roommate and his girlfriend

I got back into my van and studied the map.

Looks like the university is close by. Time to find a place to live.

Man, I don't know if I want to live with those Chinese people, I pondered as I left the apartment, I had just checked out near the UNLV campus. I needed a place to stay, but that place smelled funny. It must've been that squid or octopus, or whatever it was they were eating. Maybe I'd have better luck at the next place.

At the bottom of the stairs, I started to walk away, then suddenly stopped to reprimand myself.

What's wrong with you? You shouldn't be like that! You didn't even give those people a chance. You're supposed to be open minded. What a hypocrite.

I turned around, walked back, and knocked on the door.

"I'm interested in the room," I said quietly as the unfamiliar cooking smells wafted past me and into the desert air.

Next day, I moved in and discovered "those Chinese people" in the apartment were there for a dinner party. Only one of them lived there and he was a graduate student who taught physics at the university and was seldom home. When he was there, he liked me to help him with his English. For example, American swear words.

"What does shit mean?" my roommate asked me while eating his breakfast.

I explained that it primarily meant feces.

"That doesn't make any sense. My students often say, 'You're shitting me.' I'm not doing that to them!

"They also say, 'Don't be a pussy,' to each other. Why do they say that?"

"Um..."

He told me about his family escaping to Taiwan during China's Cultural Revolution and about the Communist Party offering a substantial reward for the capture of his father, a defecting military officer.

That experience with my Asian roommate gave me a small glimpse into a different culture. I never imagined that months later an Asian man would change my life.

It was shocking to have hundreds of students in my Economics class. The lectures took place in a theater-style auditorium, nothing like the small classrooms at Yuba or Lake Tahoe Community College. I got a D on my first quiz. Realizing university was tougher than I expected, I studied harder for the next quiz, did much better and finished with an A for the class.

Through the university I found a job as a front desk clerk at a motel within walking distance. It was a decent place but the manager, Wally, was an oddball who was always talking to himself. One day he gave me a stack of *Rent Due* notices to hand out to some tenants.

When I knocked on one door, it opened but no one was there.

"Uh, excuse me...anyone home?"

A naked lady stepped out from behind the door.

"I've been waiting," she purred seductively.

I felt my face redden.

"Umm...sorry...I'm just here to give you this," I said as I handed her the *Rent Due* notice.

"Oh, sorry. I thought you were a customer," she apologized as she shut the door.

Looking at the small stack of papers I wondered how many of the notices were for prostitutes. *What's Wally up to?*

When I knocked on doors but no one answered, I folded the notices and tucked them between the door and door frame. *Good, only one more left. Room G5.*

I found G5 and knocked. Again, the door opened with no one there. Except this time, instead of a naked lady, a ventriloquist's dummy emerged from behind the door. It wore the costume of a Vegas showgirl. Something resembling a multicolored feather duster was attached to its head.

"May I help you?" a female voice asked.

"Sorry, but I have a *Rent Due* notice for you," I said, feeling awkward.

"Just hold it in the door gap by the hinges."

I did as the dummy asked and the piece of paper was pulled from my fingers. Then the door shut.

Shaking my head, I began mumbling to myself as I walked back toward the office.

This place is too crazy. No wonder Wally is the way he is.

"What's that aroma? It smells so good," an elderly woman asked. She was sitting with her husband outside the apartment below mine as I walked down the stairs.

"Whole wheat bread. I make at least one loaf every week. Would you like some?"

"Would I ever. But I'm shocked a young man bakes bread."

"It's kind of a hobby. Plus, it saves money and tastes good."

Back in my upstairs kitchen, I sliced the loaf in half, then gave one half to my neighbor.

"Here, take these," the husband said as he handed me a stack of Burger King coupons. "Our son's the manager. They're for free Whoppers."

My vegetarianism took a vacation as I continued to supply my neighbors with fresh bread in exchange for Whopper coupons.

One day, I decided to take my panel van for a drive to visit a flea market. Ole Betsy didn't get used much in Las Vegas since I walked or rode my bicycle everywhere. As I headed toward her, I noticed she looked different and was covered in white overspray from a recent apartment building paint job. Immediately I went to the office of the apartment complex.

"Your painters covered my van with overspray when they did the building," I said to a middle-aged lady behind a desk.

"That's your van? We don't allow non-running jalopies to park at the complex."

"Who says it doesn't run? A couple of months ago I drove it all the way from Tahoe."

"I'll let the manager know what happened and he'll get back to you."

"Never mind, I'll deal with it. But if you ever need me to move my van, please let me know," I said as I walked toward the door.

On the way to the flea market, I stopped to buy some scrubbing pads then drove to a coin-operated self-serve car wash.

"Sorry 'bout that, Betsy," I said as I washed her down and scrubbed away the overspray like I was brushing an old horse.

"Non-running jalopy! How dare she. She doesn't know how I found you out in that field full o' weeds and rebuilt your engine and fixed your broken axle. Or how you sheltered me when I lived in the Sahara Tahoe parking lot. Or how you took me from Linda to Tahoe and then all the way here. Or how you'd sometimes give John a ride to work when his almost new truck wouldn't start in the winter. Yeah Betsy, you never let me down."

As I continued to murmur my one-sided conversation, I could smell strong perfume and tobacco smoke. Glancing up I noticed a big-haired middle-aged lady was staring at me, smoking a cigarette. She wore a cowgirl uniform with a nametag, *Betsy*, along with a quizzical expression. I felt a little foolish.

"Um...sorry. Betsy's my van's name."

She looked at me like I was crazy, then walked over to the change machine, shaking her head.

Maybe I am crazy. Talking to a van? But who else am I going to talk to? A showgirl dummy? Ole Betsy offered no advice.

I realized then that I didn't really have people I could talk to in Vegas. Sure, I had school and a job; I had a decent roommate and friendly neighbors. But no actual friends.

Suddenly I felt rather lonely.

Chapter Thirty-One
Seek and Find

Lange, Dorothea, photographer United States Yuba County California Marysville, 1935. Apr. U.S. Farm Security Administration Photograph. https://www.loc.gov/item/2017759582/.

But it wasn't loneliness that got me thinking about leaving Vegas. It was something deeper that I could sense without being able to name it at the time: an inner restlessness.

After hearing a presentation one day in my management class, I seriously began to doubt the wisdom of continuing my studies at the university. The professor had invited a casino executive to speak.

"I was dedicated to my success, and you should be too. I worked myself up from busboy through hard work, long hours, and study. Ten years ago, I finally received my business degree from here. I still work long hours at the casino, but now I'm the president, respected for my accomplishments and I make good money."

After the speech, I wasn't inspired to become an executive of anything. I couldn't see myself wearing a suit and tie and telling people what to do. I'd never worn a suit in my life and neckties made me feel like I was choking. I could be happy living in my van, especially if it had a heater. Why would I want to be working long hours just to make a bunch of money?

After my evening shift at the motel, I walked up a grassy knoll near my apartment and sat down. In the near distance I could see The Strip with its glitzy hotels and casinos, those towering monuments to excess and greed, as they beckoned with their garish lights and flashing neon signs. A police siren blared from afar. I just knew Las Vegas wasn't the place for a guy like me.

Leaving was no easy decision. I was doing well in my classes and had made a lot of effort to prepare for UNLV: attending community college, working, and saving my money, moving to Tahoe for Nevada State residency, studying while my roommates were skiing or partying. But something was calling me. I could hear an inner voice urging me to leave this place, to "seek and find."

I decided to leave once the Fall semester was over. I would head back to Linda for a few months, take more classes at Yuba College to at least get my two-year degree, then Betsy and I would hit the road together. I'd become a nomad, a seeker. I would try to discover where that inner voice was leading me.

When the semester ended, I typed up descriptions of swear words my roommate hadn't yet asked about, gave my bread recipe to the neighbors, and said my goodbyes. I packed my bicycle, pressure cooker, cooking utensils, box of books, and a large backpack full of clothes into Ole Betsy and began the journey back to Linda.

As I approached the California border, I thought about folk singer Woody Guthrie.

We'd been studying American singer/songwriters in my English class: Paul Simon, Bob Dylan, Guthrie, and others. We learned about "Bum Blockades" that were set up at California's borders to stop indigent migrants from entering during the Great Depression. Our professor believed that Guthrie's song, *This Land is Your Land,* was partially inspired by those unconstitutional blockades.

As I drove through Barstow, I imagined my friend Mickey's parents passing this way as kids when their families fled the Dust Bowl, as did the families of other former Linda classmates. I wondered if they were interrogated at Bum Blockades.

Driving through Bakersfield on highway 99, I thought of country singer Merle Haggard who was raised in the area. His folks were Okies too, refugees from the Dust Bowl era who settled in California. Merle was born in a converted boxcar. I started singing, "Oh, I'm proud to be an Okie from Bakersfield..."

Hmm, just doesn't have the right ring to it. No wonder he changed it to Muskogee.

In the distance I could see farm workers tending a field as it began to rain. After months of disuse the windshield wipers groaned when I hit the wiper switch. I was worried they might not work, but my fears were unfounded. Soon they were flapping rhythmically, the rubber blades and California rain washing away the desert grime. I could see ahead clearly.

As Ole Betsy hummed along homeward, I felt a huge burden lifting from my shoulders.

It was dark and still raining when I drove up the dirt road to my parents' house around 6:00 pm. It was good to have a familiar place to come home to. Too bad Charcoal our Labrador mutt had died. I'd have loved a welcome home greeting from her as I drove closer. Bizco, my dad's cross-eyed half-breed Chihuahua, yapping away was a decent Charcoal substitute when I opened the house door and walked inside.

Our Siamese cat was still alive and sleeping on a chair, but she ignored me. Mom was sitting on the couch and laid down the book she was reading. I bent down and gave her a hug. I could smell freshly baked cornbread and saw a pot of beans simmering on the Franklin wood burner.

"Where's Dad?"

"He just left to deliver tree stands."

My dad used to make Christmas tree stands from scrap wood he got from lumber mills and sell them to tree lots during the holiday season. I could never forget that one time when I was in high school, when he rented a pickup more reliable than his own, and Greg and I rode with him all the way to the San Francisco Bay Area. We were delivering tree stands a customer had ordered. When we got there, they would only pay him half the price originally agreed upon. Reluctantly he went ahead with the transaction. It was one of the few times I saw Dad cry. He barely broke even with the truck rental and all. That was a tough Christmas.

"Did you bring a turkey again?"

"Nope. That crazy motel I worked at didn't give Christmas bonuses. Got a bunch of coupons for free Whoppers though."

"That'd be different. A Burger King Christmas. Speaking of food, you must be hungry. Your dad made chili and cornbread."

"I'll get some later, I'll take a nap first. Could you ask Dad to wake me when he gets back?"

Bizco jumped around when I stood up and approached the door. He thought I was going for a ride and wanted to come along. I let him follow me to Ole Betsy and he got inside when I opened the door. He immediately lay down on the passenger seat and must have been disappointed when I didn't drive away. I crawled in back and covered myself with my sleeping bag. Bizco's ID tag and collar kept rattling as he turned round and round, trying to get comfortable. I cracked the side window open for some fresh air.

Rain fell rhythmically on the steel roof, a sound I'd someday get accustomed to throughout the Midwest and as far away as New Zealand. I closed my eyes and quickly fell asleep.

Chapter Thirty-Two
Seeking

The Wood Butcher - Marysville, California

For Christmas dinner this time, I purchased a turkey and cooked it along with other dishes as a gift to my family. With my encouragement our whole family attended a movie together at the Sutter Theater in Yuba City, something we had never done before. The movie, *Oh, God!* was funny, yet deep. I still remember the question someone asked God (George Burns): "Is Jesus Christ the son of God?"

The answer intrigued me:

"Jesus was my son. Buddha was my son. Muhammed, Moses, you, the man who said there was no room at the inn was my son."

This supported my growing impression that God's presence was universal, beyond the limits of Christianity, and that all religions teach some aspect of truth.

I got hired as a part time bartender at the Wood Butcher restaurant in Marysville and renewed my membership at the Yuba County Library to check out books on philosophy and alternative religions.

Since I was busy with work and taking Welding and Earth Science courses at the community college, I'd ask my mother to read the spiritual books, then give me a synopsis of their contents.

One day at the library I saw two books sitting on a table, one titled *Edible Seaweed* and the other about sailing. Glancing through them, I was intrigued. *Maybe that's what I should do, live on a sailboat?* After checking them out I managed to find time to read *those* books and eventually every book the library had about sailing. I also joined a Sailing Book of the Month Club. Over a dozen sailing books soon sat on a makeshift bookshelf in my trailer.

After memorizing all the parts of a sailboat and various nautical terms, studying celestial navigation, and carrying pieces of rope in my pocket to practice knot-tying, at one point I realized the futility of my efforts. *I'll never learn sailing this way. I've got to get to the ocean. How can I do that?* Marysville was at least a two-hour drive from the ocean.

The answer came at the Wood Butcher.

A local fellow would occasionally stop by the restaurant for a beer and tell me stories about working on his brother's fishing boat in Kodiak, Alaska during the summer.

That sounded enthralling. *I could do that. Move to Alaska and work on a fishing boat, learn about the ocean and make good money.*

But what about Candice?

Candice worked at the Wood Butcher too. She was from Santa Cruz and had recently graduated from the university there. She worked part time as a waitress at the restaurant, was smart, cute, and best of all, she liked me. I was smitten. We went on many dates, but I was also stuck in an existential quagmire. Should I continue my quest for truth and adventure by going to Alaska, or should I stay in Marysville and settle down with Candice?

I expressed my concerns in a poem and read it to her.

After hearing my poem, Candice answered my "stay or go" question by seldom talking to me again, for reasons that never became clear to me. Was I too serious about our relationship? Or not serious enough? Or maybe she wanted someone who was a better poet?

Feeling rather dejected I wrote to my cousin Gretchen, who lived in Juneau, and told her my plans to come to Alaska. She wrote back and explained she didn't actually live in Juneau, but on a nearby island. To get there I'd need to hitch a boat ride from Juneau.

Just keep asking around at the docks. Someone will be heading nearby and give you a ride. You might even find a job. I heard you're a good cook. Captains like good cooks onboard.

With renewed determination I worked extra hard to be physically ready for working on a fishing boat: riding my bicycle to work and school, jogging, jumping rope, and lifting weights at the college gym. Inside my trailer, I'd sleep on a piece of plywood instead of a mattress. As my hair and beard grew out, I began to look more like a fisherman instead of a clean-cut casino busboy.

Meanwhile my insatiable curiosity led me to read popular books like *Chariots of the Gods* whose thesis was that aliens visited earth centuries ago and *The Late Great Planet Earth* that tried to predict (unsuccessfully) the world's end times. Their insights failed to impress me.

My mother continued to review other spiritually inclined library books for me and instead of running away to hide, I listened, at least for a bit, to the Jehovah's Witnesses and Mormon missionaries when they visited, and even paid attention to a Baptist preacher who stopped by one day to invite us to church. Although none of their ideas moved my heart, or mind, the sincere dedication of these devout visitors impressed me and made me want to find something to believe in.

Admittedly, I had an anti-Christian chip on my shoulder. So much so that on Sunday mornings when the local after-church crowd came to the Wood Butcher for food and drink I didn't have a particularly good attitude. Especially when they kept ordering time-consuming blender drinks like Ramos Gin Fizzes. Grumbling to myself, I washed out yet another blender pitcher.

In charge of background music, I would often intentionally play the Crosby, Stills & Nash song *Cathedral,* which is laced with anti-Christian sentiment, for example, claiming that too many people lied in the name of Christ. Nobody ever complained.

Where Do We Go from Here?
Where do we go from here?
Do we walk love's rocky path,
perhaps stumble
And bruise our hearts on stones thrown
by jagged illusions of what love should be?
Where do we go from here?
As youth withers and dreams fade
Into reality.
Where does that path lead?

Up mountains, down valleys
Through tempest, storm and wind,
As ravens cackle?
Or through fields of butterflies and ladybugs
Where white doves coo?
Where do I go from here?
Seek...seek and find?
Or gamble on picket fence
And nine to five?
Bob Gauper - 1977

Chapter Thirty-Three
Sunshine and Magpies

God became real to me in an unlikely place, my Earth Science class. I enrolled in the class primarily to learn about weather and the ocean. However, the intricacies of Earth's ecosystem, and how everything in the universe worked together, amazed me.

I can't even make a pitching machine that works properly. Someone/something had to have designed this.

Nearly every night, I slept outside my trailer on a small cot in a good down sleeping bag which kept me warm on cold nights, only going inside when it rained. Frequently waterfowl flying overhead would lull me to sleep as they called out above the heavy fog. On clear nights, I'd stare at the endless stars, and I was enthralled at the vastness of the universe.

How can anyone see this and not believe in a Creator?

In Earth Science class we also learned about Copernicus, Giordano Bruno, Galileo and other scientists and deep thinkers who were persecuted by the Roman Catholic Church for their beliefs.

Where's that new truth now? Where are the people being persecuted for their ground-breaking beliefs? Deeper understanding must be out there, but where?

Taped to the wall in my trailer was a quote by Henry David Thoreau:

If a man does not keep pace with his companions, perhaps it is because he hears a different drummer. Let him step to the music which he hears, however measured or far away.

I sure felt like someone who couldn't keep pace with his companions. I remember telling Candice once, "I sure wish I could just be like other guys and accept my life as it is."

But Socrates had taught that the unexamined life was not worth living.

While contemplating Thoreau's quote, a song by the Moody Blues crackled on my beat-up radio. It sounded something like:

I gave you the forests and flowers to play with...Why am I so alone?

Was God alone and if so, why? I pondered.

That night, after gazing at the star-filled sky, I closed my eyes and asked God what I should do with my life. Seconds after opening them a bright star shot across the Milky Way. In the morning, after being awakened by the sunshine and magpies flying overhead, I wrote a poem apologizing to God for the suffering we might have caused.

With a lump in my throat, I sold Ole Betsy. We'd been through a lot together. It was like saying goodbye to an old friend, but it was time to venture down a new path, a path that my old primer brown panel truck couldn't take.

After selling, or giving away, nearly everything else I owned until all my possessions could fit into a backpack, I was ready to be a wayfarer.

My mom continued to research library books for me. Usually none of them warranted much attention until one day...

"Bobby, here's something interesting. It's a religion called Baha'i, about the unity of mankind and all major religions coming from one God. They also talk about the harmony of science and religion. I'm interested in that even if you're not. There's a flyer here, maybe you could give them a call."

Later that day I called the number on the pamphlet to ask for more information. A man answered.

"We're having a fireside chat in a few days. That would be a good time to visit. Where are you calling from?"

"Marysville."

"We don't have any active members in that area. We're in Grass Valley. You're welcome to visit us here."

"I'll think about it. Thanks for the invitation."

Normally I would be willing to drive forty-five minutes from Linda to Grass Valley in my search for universal truth, but since I'd already sold Ole Betsy, the prospect was unrealistic.

I made a replica of a hand with an oversized thumb out of stiff cardboard, painted it fluorescent pink, then attached it to a collapsible automotive antenna from a wrecking yard. Attached to my backpack, it would catch the attention of passing motorists as I walked down the road. (During my future travels, people would confirm it was indeed the bright pink cardboard hand that inspired them to stop and pick me up.)

Early one morning, as the spring of 1978 was turning to warm summer, my dad gave me a ride to Highway 70 near Marysville High School and dropped me off. With my backpack leaning against a traffic sign, the cardboard hand solicited rides for me while I sat down to read Carlos Castaneda's *The Teachings of Don Juan*. My first stop would be Rogue River, Oregon, where David, a friend from Tahoe, now lived.

Before long, someone stopped to pick me up and once again, I was leaving Linda.

Chapter Thirty-Four
A Leap of Faith

Blind men and an elephant - 1916 - Illustrator unknown, Public domain, via Wikimedia Commons

The cardboard thumb was sure working out well, I reflected, walking toward a traffic sign that looked like a good resting spot on the onramp to I-5 in Medford. It was around 5:00 p.m. and Rogue River wasn't far away. It was nice getting so many rides so quickly, but I'd barely read any of *The Teachings of Don Juan*.

Seconds after that thought, a car pulled in front of me.

"Where you headin'?" a young lady asked through the opened passenger window.

"Uh, Alaska, but first, Rogue River."

"Hop in. You're almost there."

"Where you stayin' in Rogue River? I know the area well."

"With David Dodge on Ford Road."

"David Dodge on Ford Road, that's funny. I know where that is. It's about ten, fifteen minutes outa town. Sorry I can't take you all the way there. I'd be late for my appointment in Grants Pass."

"That's okay. I'll just give him a call."

As it happened, my friend David Dodge picked me up in his Dodge truck and took me to his parents' house on Ford Road.

After helping my old friend build a river rock fireplace, I hitched a ride to Portland and got a room for the night in a cheap hotel. It was a narrow place with barely enough room for a twin bed and chest of drawers. A small window was open, and it was raining hard. Six stories below, the tops of umbrellas were lined up and moving back and forth next to the street. At the sound of squeaky brakes, the umbrellas closed in unison revealing their owners who stepped onto a bus. A small puff of black diesel smoke exited the bus's tailpipe as it pulled away from the street. Although I'd only been in Portland a few hours, it was the longest time I'd ever spent downtown in a large city. A normal city, that is. Las Vegas didn't count.

In keeping with my usual practice, I unrolled my sleeping pad and bag on the floor and lay down for a good night's sleep. Early next morning, it was still raining and instead of hitch-hiking to Seattle, I took Amtrak.

Thankfully, it wasn't raining in Seattle. Right away I got a room at the YMCA, stored my backpack, then walked to the waterfront to see about catching a ferry to Alaska.

"Try back in a couple days," the ticket agent mumbled after telling me there weren't any tickets available. That was disappointing, but not overly troubling. After the experience of breaking down in Crescent City, I was determined to enjoy my traveling experience and not worry excessively about the destination.

Then something happened that would change my life, something I had never imagined.

A young man was standing nearby handing out fliers.

"Join us for an International Dinner and learn about new ideas," he said enthusiastically as he handed me a flier, a short distance from the ticket booth. He looked to be in his early twenties, stocky with short black hair, and wearing a cheap-looking checkered dress shirt with dark slacks. If it weren't for the checkered shirt and the lack of a badge reading *Elder So-and-so,* he could have been a Mormon missionary.

I glanced at the flier, stuck it in my shirt pocket and walked away.

Hmmm, new ideas. Plus, the flier said dinner is free. Might check it out. Not much else to do. Looks like I'm stuck in Seattle for at least a couple of extra days anyway.

After playing tourist and walking around the waterfront for a couple of hours I went back to my room. Sitting on the bed, I fingered the International Dinner flier, feeling tired and not really inclined to go anywhere. But I was also hungry. *Don't be shy. Maybe you'll meet some nice people.* There was a map on the flier with directions. Looked easy enough.

A short walk up some hilly streets took me to the house where the dinner was to take place. It had a large picture window in front through which, from the street, I could see several people inside. Surprisingly, I wasn't anxious about going in, but rather had an uncanny feeling that I was supposed to be there.

A friendly young lady opened the door shortly after I knocked.

"Please come in. Who invited you?"

"Didn't catch his name. Met him by the waterfront. Black hair, built like a football player."

"Sounds like Peter. I'll go find him."

Seconds later he arrived.

"Wow. I'm so glad you could make it. What inspired you to come?"

"Free dinner! Honestly, although my plans are to go to Alaska, I'm keeping an open mind to new experiences. You could say I'm on a quest."

"For what?"

"Truth. Spiritual enlightenment."

"Well, you've come to the right place."

"What group is ...?"

"Okay everyone. Let's gather around in a circle and please state your name and where you're from," announced a man slightly older than most of the others.

It was impressive to hear all the different states and countries people called home. California, Montana, New Jersey, North Dakota, New York, Australia, Japan, Germany, Korea and many others.

After the introductions they started serving dinner. It looked like pretty simple fare. Rice and vegetables with thin strips of beef.

A short Japanese man stood up in front of everyone. "Hello, my name is Sato-San, and I will be part of the entertainment this evening while you enjoy your meal."

He started walking and talking like a robot. Although most of what he was saying was unintelligible, he was entertaining.

Peter sang a song. A little off key, but full of passion.

A young lady, who looked like a nun with her short hair and modest clothing, strummed a guitar and sang Bob Dylan's folk song, *Blowin' in the Wind*. She changed the lyrics of the familiar refrain to:

The answer, my friends is in the hearts of men...

which seemed a little odd, although it made more sense than finding answers in the wind.

Then there was a talk about blind men and an elephant, along with a slide show and an invitation to attend a weekend workshop in the mountains to hear more. In fact, a van would be leaving in a couple of hours.

"Sign me up," I told Peter. "I'll miss out on using my room at the Y. But since I can't get a ferry ticket to Alaska for a couple of days, I might as well go to your workshop."

"Wow. That's great!" He looked a bit shocked that I wanted to go. "I'll go get a signup form."

As I started filling out paperwork, three guys visiting from New Zealand approached me.

"We overheard you saying you couldn't get a ticket to Alaska. We're booked on the ferry tomorrow, but Tim here has a family emergency and can't go. He can sell you his ticket, and you can join us."

"Okay. That sounds even better than going to this workshop. I'll tell Peter I've changed my mind and go with you guys."

Peter seemed disappointed when I told him my change of plans.

"But this could change your life! You said you're searching for enlightenment. Maybe God wants you to go."

God? This is about God? That's why these people look like missionaries. They are.

"I'm sorry Peter. But I can't believe my luck in getting a ticket to Alaska. I might be stuck in Seattle for weeks. Running into those guys must be why I felt compelled to come to this dinner."

Peter left, then seconds later the man that had presented the blind men and elephant lecture, sat down beside me.

"Hi. My name's Tom. Peter tells me you've changed your mind about attending our workshop. He also said you're on a spiritual journey. Perhaps you should take a leap of faith. Alaska will still be there when you get back. In fact, our movement has fishing boats there you might be able to work on."

What should I do? Alaska or the workshop? The words, "Take a leap of faith," kept repeating in my mind. *Okay, I'll go to the workshop.* The first people I told were the New Zealanders.

"Guys, I've decided to go to the workshop. Hope you have a great trip to Alaska. Who knows, maybe we'll run into each other there."

Peter soon reappeared and gladly received my workshop form along with the nominal fee. Hours later we were packed into a van and before long we were leaving the city.

The van driver gushed, "I think it's time to sing a song." He started singing *You are my Sunshine.* The missionary types joined in.

A skinny guy with a long beard was sitting behind me. He rolled his eyes and I responded, briefly shaking my head.

Little did I know that this workshop was about to alter the trajectory of my life.

Chapter Thirty-Five

Choo Choo Pow!

Old Swedish locomotive - 1925-1927, Tekniska museet Stockholm, Public domain, via Wikimedia Commons {{PD-1996}}

After what seemed like a couple of hours, the van arrived at a large cabin. Although it was dark, the outline of a mountain range was visible, and I could hear a river running nearby. The fresh smell of pine trees filled the air.

Tom, who must have been in another vehicle, approached the van.

"Men, sleep in the bedroom upstairs. There're people already sleeping so be as quiet as possible. We start exercise at 7:00. Someone will be around to wake you up."

I took my backpack and sleeping bag upstairs and looked around the room. There were four people already sleeping and one was snoring loudly. I found some room on the floor as far away from the snorer as possible and unrolled my sleeping pad and bag. It had been a long and eventful day. Within seconds, I fell asleep.

Around 6:40 am I was already awake when I heard singing outside the bedroom door. It was a cheerful song about a red, red robin bob-bob-bobbin along.

I got up, dressed, and went downstairs. Peter was there.

"When you're done in the bathroom join us for morning exercise. You'll be able to see us through the bedroom window."

After washing, I went back upstairs to hang up my towel and looked out onto a small field where around fifteen people had gathered. By the time I made it downstairs several more had joined the group.

"Okay, everyone!" an enthusiastic fellow led the interesting morning ritual. "Before we start exercises, let's make a circle. We're going to do a *choo choo pow!* All you do is make the sound of a train engine while moving your arms like train wheels. After nine *choo-choos,* raise your arms and shout, *yeah yeah pow!*

Here goes! *Choo-choo-choo, choo-choo-choo, choo-choo-choo, yeah yeah pow!* See, that wasn't so hard, was it? Let's do it one more time.

Choo-choo-choo…"

I watched with skepticism.

Hmm. Okay, this is weird. Choo choo pow?

What have I gotten myself into? Seems like something elementary school children would do. Harmless enough, though. Oh, what the heck.

Half-heartedly, I joined in. It got easier for me when they started more normal exercises like jumping jacks and toe-touches.

Afterward, a simple breakfast of homemade muesli and orange juice was served. I really wanted a hot cup of coffee, but none was available. Instead, we drank lukewarm, weak cocoa.

After breakfast it was time for our first lecture.

I could hear singing inside the cabin and as I entered, I saw around twenty young adults gathered. Soon, more joined. Three people were at the front of the room leading the singing. Two were playing guitars.

Most of the music was American folk songs. *If I had a hammer, This Land is Your Land, Country Roads* and of course *In the Hearts of Men,* a.k.a. *Blowin' in the Wind,* and others.

The music was nice, but I wasn't that interested in singing; I was mostly curious about the message they had to offer.

Although the audience was more diverse and the songs weren't about Jesus, it made me uncomfortable. It reminded me of the Pentecostal church services I used to attend with Mickey and the rest of my baseball team.

"Praise Jesus! Praise Jesus!" women in the congregation shouted as they raised their arms during the worship music.

"Praise Jesus!" They continued as the music stopped and Pastor Booth stepped forward to preach, his face and bald head oozing with sweat as he shouted for us to repent of our sins and accept Jesus as our personal Savior.

"Get washed in the blood! Get washed in the blood of Jesus!"

"Hallelujah! Praise the Lord!" the women continued as if they were in a trance.

Then came the altar call.

"Come forward and give your life to Jesus!"

Mickey's mother stood up then glanced over to us, motioning with her head for us to follow her. Mickey and his brothers obliged while I stayed in the pew. An old woman sitting in front of me turned around and stared at me scornfully. I still didn't budge.

Maybe if my neighbor Fred, who attended this church, was a better person, I'd go up there. And if those guys up at the altar weren't always stealing stuff.

Nope. Not gonna happen. Not goin' up there to be 'saved'.

The only thing that stopped me from turning and walking out was the thought of the potluck afterward, and Mickey's mom's fried chicken.

Just like back then, I wasn't going to follow something because of emotion, or peer pressure.

Finally, the music stopped and Tom, the guy that convinced me to go to the workshop, walked to the front of the room and stood next to a large chalkboard.

"Would you like to know your purpose in life? To know why you are here, to know why that river and the beautiful mountains and trees outside are here? I'm going to teach you the purpose of creation."

Love.

That's what Tom's lecture boiled down to. All of creation, including me, was made to give and receive love. It made sense. Even the Bible quotes, especially Romans 1:20, which I scribbled into my diary:

Romans 1:20 – know God's invisible nature in the stuff He made.

Wow. That's the first time I ever paid attention to a Bible quote.

While pleasantly surprised to find myself looking forward to the next lecture, I intentionally came late to miss the singing.

Eve had sex with an angel? I'm supposed to believe this stuff?

Along with some of the other guests, I almost walked out. I remembered the Adam and Eve story from the Sunday School I occasionally attended in Linda. An angel disguised as a snake tempted Eve to eat an apple even though God told her not to. Then she shared it with Adam, and they were so ashamed, they covered their lower parts with fig leaves (which I'd always thought must have been super itchy, based on the fig tree in our yard) and that's why the world was so messed up. I didn't believe the apple story back then and wasn't impressed with the R-rated version. I squirmed in my seat as Tom continued talking about Lucifer, archangels, and other stuff that I did not understand and was not that interested in. It was a relief when the talk was over.

Next came a lecture where we heard that Jesus was the second Adam whose task was to restore what I came to think of as Adam and Eve's literal screw-up. However, Jesus didn't get much support, not even from John the Baptist, and the Jews and Roman authorities weren't enamored with him turning over tables in the temple, calling himself a king and all that, so they killed him. As one might imagine, I wasn't that interested in the Jesus story either.

At the end of the day, I began to doubt if I should even be at the workshop. I could have left that evening but didn't.

The next day's educational session began with a lesson on the parallels of Jewish and Christian history, which I did find interesting, especially when Tom said God inspired prophets and religious leaders from *all* religions in preparation for the coming of Christ. However, Jesus hadn't completed his mission and needed to return. Based on the historical parallels, Jesus *had* returned and in the next and final lecture for the weekend, we'd find out where.

I quickly ate lunch, went to my room and lay down. There were so many things to ponder, it felt like my mind was ready to explode. Although I was resistant toward most of the biblical teachings, I began to realize my own arrogance. I was working toward being a thoroughly educated person but knew almost nothing about Judeo-Christian history. Tom's knowledge and presentation were impressive.

Jesus returned? If that's true, then my neighbor Fred and Pastor Booth should have flown up in the air to meet him on the clouds like they always said they would. A few days before leaving Linda I saw Fred driving his tractor.

But Tom taught a different idea about how Jesus would return. He'd come back as a man born on the earth, and Korea was the special nation where Tom said the messiah would be born.

Many Koreans had become devout Christians and were anxiously awaiting the returning Lord. Prior to the communist takeover of Pyongyang, North Korea's largest city, was often called the Jerusalem of the East. Though the "Hermit Kingdom" had endured brutal occupation from 1905 to 1945 by the Japanese who forbade Christian worship, the Korean people remained faithful. The division of Korea at the 38th parallel into communist and democratic countries represented the separation of good and evil where God would finally triumph over Satan through the Messiah.

After the lecture I walked down to the river to be alone, but my solitude was short-lived.

"Hey man. Did you know these people are the Moonies?" said Mark who had suddenly appeared beside me.

"How do you know that?"

"I asked Tom and he confirmed it."

Moonies? I knew hardly anything about the group, except something about kidnapping and brainwashing, but these people seemed pretty darn harmless. Although Tom encouraged guests to stay longer for the following week-long workshop, they definitely weren't forcing anyone to stick around. In fact, once the lecture was over, it looked like nearly everyone, including me, was getting ready to leave.

Chapter Thirty-Six
Finding

It was Sunday evening.

Laden with my fully loaded backpack in the parking area, I suddenly stopped. The van heading back to Seattle was about ten steps away. Ten steps to continue my journey to Alaska. To my right were the staff members and guests who were staying for the week-long workshop. Most of them looked sad as they watched the van fill up with people who were leaving. Especially Peter, who was also about ten steps away.

Mark, the long-haired skinny guy who had rolled his eyes at *You are my Sunshine*, motioned to me from inside the van. Peter pleaded with his eyes for me to stay. *Ten steps.* My heart racing, I glanced left then right.

Van...Peter...Van...Peter?

Breathing deeply, I closed my eyes, then reopened them. The driver looked anxious to leave. Something made me turn and walk toward Peter. Mark slammed the door shut on the van and my alternative destiny. We all watched as the vehicle meandered down the dirt road toward the big city.

"Wow, that was close. We were praying you'd stay. How'd you decide?" asked Peter.

"Don't really know. Just felt I needed to stay. Now what?"

"Time to take a break. It's been an intense weekend. Put your pack back in your room and stay there reading, or take a nap, or go for a walk by the river. Make sure you're back here in about an hour though. Dinner's at seven. Helen's making raspberry shortcake."

Upstairs, instead of wall-to-wall sleeping bags on the bedroom floor, there were only four. Pulling my diary out of my backpack I began writing:

What an intense two days. Still struggling with all the Bible and Jesus stuff. That's why I wanted to leave. Don't want to change my attitude towards Christianity. What Tom said about not taking the Bible literally was helpful. Also, I liked what he said about God operating throughout history through prophets, philosophers, and scientists. It helped clarify my own theories that God works through all religions. He probably works through Christianity too. I need to lighten up...

"Wake up, sleepyhead," Peter whispered.

The squiggly line trailing away from an unfinished sentence revealed I had fallen asleep while writing.

"Uh...hi. What's up?"

"It's dinner time. We're gathering downstairs."

"Okay, but can I ask you a question?"

"Sure."

"Why do people keep calling you Mike? Isn't your name Peter?"

"No time now. I'll tell you later."

The strains of John Denver's song *Country Roads* drifted up through the stairwell (a song my future wife would grow to hate, but more about that later).

Great. More singing.

As we walked downstairs the music stopped and Randall, a fundamentalist Christian from Australia, said a blessing for the dinner.

The main course was forgettable, but dessert looked divine. Raspberry shortcake: fresh raspberries with berry syrup, whipped cream, and homemade shortcake. It reminded me of the strawberry shortcake my dad used to make. For a moment I pictured myself sitting in my dad's large strawberry patch eating fresh berries with a bowl of sweetened milk.

"Where'd you get fresh raspberries?" I asked Peter. "Seldom see them where I'm from. There's tons of blackberries though."

"We pick 'em at a farm about thirty minutes from here. We'll probably go there sometime."

As I savored my dessert, I realized I hadn't cooked anything for myself in nearly a week, which was unusual.

There were around a dozen people in the dining room. Only six of us, including me, seemed to be guests. There was a long-haired liberal hippie type from Tacoma, a Christian from Germany who was constantly arguing about Bible passages, a struggling Christian from Oregon whose dad was a Pentecostal preacher, a young woman from Seattle, Randall, and myself.

Around thirty guests had been at the weekend workshop. I wondered what compelled these ones to stay. Maybe it was completely practical. If I had a job or school to return to, I might have left also.

After dinner I went outside, walked to the nearby river, and sat on a large boulder. A woodpecker pecked a tree, searching for food. *Click click click!* Its rapping echoed throughout the forest. The evening sky was still bright, but the woodlands were getting dark. A three-quarter moon began to appear behind a ragged mountain peak. I took deep breaths of pine-scented mountain air, feeling at peace and happy I had made the decision to stay longer in this place that felt like paradise.

The following days were less intense than the weekend. In addition to listening to lectures and discussing their contents, I helped out in the kitchen, worked on clearing a path to the river and deep cleaning the workshop site. One day ten of us went on a hike.

It was different from any hike I'd ever been on. We climbed up tree roots that were growing out of the mountainside, ascending higher and higher until, after about thirty minutes, we reached a waterfall. There we stopped for a brief rest before continuing onward.

About an hour later, we reached our destination, a crystal-clear alpine lake surrounded by mountain peaks. I recognized one distinctive peak I had seen from the workshop site.

"Look," Peter called out while pointing at one of the pinnacles. "Mountain goats."

Someone had brought binoculars and passed them around. As I gazed at the agile animals clinging to the mountainside, a raindrop fell on the lens.

"We'd better have lunch before it starts raining hard," Helen suggested. "We usually sit over there by those boulders. For dessert you can pick wild blueberries. They're every-where."

Helen was kind and motherly, her blond hair short and nun-like, similar to other women I had met at the International Dinner in Seattle; but her light blue eyes had a distinctive sparkle.

As we ate our lunch, it began to drizzle. Helen said, "A little fire would sure be nice. Next time I'll bring matches."

Less than five minutes after her statement, two fit-looking, clean-cut young men who could have been military, or perhaps casino barboys, suddenly appeared from a nearby trail. They walked over and chatted briefly with our group, then left. Minutes later, they reappeared with armloads of wood, built us a small campfire, then disappeared back down the mountain. We would never see them again.

"I think they were angels," Helen said softly, rubbing her hands in front of the fire.

"Oh," I responded, taken aback. It was certainly inexplicable that strangers would make that hard trek up the mountainside just to build us a fire. Too bad she hadn't asked for coffee.

The workshop continued as we learned more about God's purpose for creation, hu-mankind's fall from grace, and God's work in history to restore the original ideal. We also learned that these ideas originated from a teacher who had started out in a cardboard hut in war-torn South Korea and built a worldwide movement which promoted peace and religious unity. His name was Sun Myung Moon.

Some of the teachings were challenging for me, but many of these new ideas made sense. In addition, not only was my mind growing, so was my heart as I began to feel a deeper appreciation for God's children and His creation. The "missionary types" impressed me with their love for God, unselfishness, and dedication to a higher purpose. I wanted to be like them.

Nevertheless, by Thursday, I still couldn't decide what to do with this new information and the new feelings that accompanied it. Upstairs, while contemplating my next move, I closed my eyes and asked God what I should do. To my utter surprise I heard a voice.

"Bob!" Silence.

Wow. This can't be. God is speaking to me?

"Bob. Could you throw down my swimming trunks?" It was Peter, or Mike, calling from outside.

What a disappointment. I brought Peter his trunks and joined him for a swim in the frigid river.

That night, before going to sleep, I asked God again what I should do. No voices called out my name, but I had a dream.

In that dream I was sitting inside a garbage dumpster surrounded and covered with filth. The stench was unbearable and no matter how hard I tried to escape; my efforts were in vain. I felt worthless, like the garbage enveloping me. Suddenly, I heard noises overhead and saw a giant version of Sun Myung Moon towering over me, smiling brightly. He was like the Jolly Green Giant, except for being Asian and not green. He reached down, pulled me from the dumpster and placed me gently on the ground.

In the morning my pillow was soaked with tears, and I was at peace, embraced in God's love. It suddenly seemed clear to me that much of my adult life had been leading up to this point. I told Peter I would stay on for another week.

A few days after my dream, although I cringed at the thought of looking like a clean-cut casino worker again, I swallowed my pride and asked Helen if she would kindly give me a haircut and shave my beard.

That was when I decided to become a full-time member of Reverend Moon's movement which, at the time, was known as the Unification Church.

I had no idea of the excitement, joy, but also suffering and sadness that would follow that momentous choice.

Chapter Thirty-Seven
Brother Bob

Bust of a Monk - 1400's - Martin Schongauer, Public domain, via Wikimedia Commons

Eventually the American branch of the Unification Movement would develop influential newspapers, science conferences, schools, colleges and think tanks. But back in the 1970s when I joined, Reverend Moon's organization was still in its pioneering phase. We mostly needed two things: people, and funds. Consequently, a new recruit like me had a choice of two missions: witnessing (as Peter had witnessed to me) or fundraising.

After spending several weeks at the mountain retreat listening to talks, picking raspberries, helping in the kitchen, meeting new guests and enjoying nature, I felt like I had become a monk after all, especially when people called me Brother Bob.

Reverend Moon's teachings opened my heart to Jesus. Now that I was a religious nut, I figured it was about time I learned more about Christ. So, I started with the basics. I found a children's Bible at one of our church centers and began reading it. I also kept a New Testament in my shirt pocket that I would often consult. Furthermore, I started studying *"The Imitation of Christ"* (a Christian devotional book composed by Thomas Kempis in the early 1400's), and was especially moved by the chapter, *"Few love the cross of Christ"* where I read the following passage: *"Jesus always has many who love His Heavenly kingdom, but few who bear His cross...Many love Him as long as they encounter no hardship; many praise and bless Him as long as they receive some comfort from Him."*

Soon, I was asked to join the witnessing team in Seattle. Peter, a.k.a. Mike, would be my mentor.

We were a good team. I was filled with the child-like spirit of a new member and Peter had wisdom and experience. He was also fearless in approaching people and we were always bringing new guests. Many were inspired by the teachings and lifestyle, but not enough to dedicate their lives to a new movement.

Suddenly, Peter was no longer around (I found out later he was kidnapped by his mother), and I began working with others or on my own. Finally, a young engineer from Holland decided to stay and join our little community; soon, others followed. I was ecstatic and probably a bit arrogant. Then the universe or some other invisible force proceeded to show me that it wasn't all about me, and for a while I couldn't seem to convince anyone to even come to dinner to hear the elephant story.

Tom suggested I might do better on the fundraising team. To my surprise, I was good at it.

"Turn left here!" yelled Stephen.

"I can't turn left, it's a one-way street!"

Stephen grew up in the Bronx and although he was in his early twenties, had never driven a car. Meanwhile, I was twenty-four and had been driving since my early teens when a friend's dad gave me a barely running Fiat.

But even though I had been in the driver's seat for over nine years, I had almost no experience with big-city driving. I hadn't even parallel parked; yet here I was, driving a full-sized van throughout Portland, Oregon, having directions shouted at me from a guy that didn't know about one-way streets.

Stephen and I were part of a larger fundraising team from the Seattle area Unification Church. Since I was one of only a few that had a United States driver's license I was designated the "sub-team" driver, the sub-team consisting of me and Stephen.

We were *so* different.

He grew up in the Bronx and spoke so fast and with an accent so strong I often couldn't understand him. He also seemed to always be in a hurry. He reminded me of the skinny jackrabbits I used to shoot with my .22 rifle in the Dredger Ponds.

"What's your goal for tonight? Mine's a hundred dollars," blurted Stephen.

"Goal?"

"Yeah. How much money you tryin' to make?"

"I don't know, I just joined the church. My goal is a bit more basic. Like...not leaving. Not sure I can handle this fundraising stuff."

"You'd be surprised. It's often quite exciting. You'll get used to it."

"I'm not sure it's something I wanna get used to. But I promised I would stick with it for twenty-one days. Only eighteen more to go."

"If I can figure out how to get there, let's go to the Hilton. I have a plan."

Eventually we were in the Hilton Hotel parking lot.

"This is a kick-out so we have to be careful," he said, grabbing several bundles of roses from the van.

"Kick-out?"

"Yes. They don't let us sell here. If a manager or security guard sees us, they'll kick us out. Here, take these flowers and hide them under your jacket. I'll hide some under mine. When we get inside, follow me to the cocktail lounge then watch what I do."

I followed Stephen to the lounge and stood near the doorway, watching in astonishment as he dropped to his knees and disappeared under an unoccupied table. For a short time, I had no idea where he was, until his head popped up near a table of people who were soon shaking their heads. I chuckled as this continued throughout the bar. Instead of jackrabbits, he now reminded me of the ground squirrels that popped up on my parents' rural California acreage.

However, at one table Stephen stood up. I could see him talking to someone and nodding his head. He then bolted over to me.

"We need to give a rose to every woman in the bar. You start on the left side of the room, and I'll start on the right. They're already paid for."

Once every woman in the bar had a rose, we quickly walked outside the hotel and ran to the van. (Like I said, he was always in a hurry.)

Inside the van, Stephen gushed, "You'll never believe what just happened! Evel Knievel bought all those flowers! He gave me a one- hundred-dollar bill and told me to keep the change! A hundred dollars, that was my goal!"

I was skeptical.

"Evel Knievel, the famous daredevil? Yeah, right."

"That's who the people at his table said he was."

I started driving toward the exit and this doubting Thomas soon had an attitude adjustment. In the back of the parking lot sat a semi-truck trailer sporting a huge graphic: *America's Daredevil - Evel Knievel.*

Exciting?

Stephen was right about that. He was also right about me getting used to fundraising. I kept my promise of staying on the team for twenty-one days and would eventually spend many memorable years on the Unification Church's national-level Mobile Fundraising team (MFT). During those years, I never once crawled under tables in a Hilton Hotel cocktail lounge, but only because there weren't too many Hiltons where I was eventually stationed.

Oh, and I also accomplished my goal of not leaving the Church.

Chapter Thirty-Eight

Million Dollar Experience

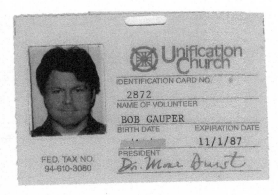

"It was a million-dollar experience that I wouldn't give a nickel to do again."

I could relate with that Vietnam Vet when I heard him on the radio. Having spent over five years as a member of the Unification Church's Mobile Fundraising Team (MFT) I had similar sentiments.

For example, I believe we worked too hard. Jews are commanded in the Torah to take a weekly day of rest. Even their servants and animals are to do likewise. Most MFT members did not have that luxury. Some blame that on the "Banzai" spirit of many of the Japanese leaders.

After twenty-one days of fundraising for the Seattle church, I had some idea of what I was getting myself into when I agreed to Tom's suggestion for me to join National MFT. A couple of days after our conversation he gave me a plane ticket to Kansas City and drove me to the airport.

Somewhere in the countryside near Kansas City, I took part in a three-day workshop attended by seasoned MFT veterans and new recruits. It felt like a meeting of the United Nations with people from all over the world: Africa, Australia, Asia, Canada, Europe, South America, and even Linda, California.

It was an exciting workshop with lectures on the importance of the time we were living in, Reverend Moon's life and his work to unite Christianity against atheistic communism.

One especially moving moment was when Andrew, a European church member, shared his testimony of how he escaped Russia after his family was murdered by communist thugs. He watched his family being torched to death.

As the workshop was winding down, the lecturer shouted:

"Who can stay this course for one year!?"

The crowd, most of whom had leapt to their feet, shouted, "We can!"

"Two years?"

"We can!!"

"Three years?"

"We can!!"

That's what most of the audience shouted. As for me, based on past experiences at the Pentecostal Church in Linda, I had developed a healthy skepticism regarding anything that resembled mass hysteria. Remaining calmly in my seat, I quietly vowed to do my best. I already knew it wouldn't be easy, but how could I complain when there were people suffering in the world, like Andrew and his family?

When the training was over, all of us received assignments to various regions around the nation. My assignment was the Midwest, coincidentally where my parents were from, or rather, had *escaped* from. I worked briefly in Milwaukee in late November of 1978 before being sent to Minneapolis.

∞

Christianity depicts hell as a place of unbearable heat. They obviously didn't work outside in the middle of winter in that God-forsaken freezer of North America commonly known as Minnesota.

Minus ten. I can still see that number flashing on a digital bank sign near the Kmart parking lot, like some evil tormenter. The sign would flash:

-10... -10... -10... -10... as if to say:

You get to fundraise the Kmart parking lot in -10 degrees Fahrenheit. Idiot! Go back to California!

It was a long time before I made it back to California. I was somehow able to survive MFT for over five years. There were good days, bad days, unfathomably horrible and immensely joyful days. It was something like going to war.

On one of those horrible days, I had been going shop-to-shop peddling flowers, or whatever, in Minneapolis. No one was donating, and I was getting persecuted everywhere. The weight of the world seemed to be on my shoulders. I sat down on a bench in a small park to have a pity party. My head was resting on my hands as I stared at the ground looking for worms to eat, when a white Labrador dog startled me and began licking my ear and wagging its tail. Standing next to the dog was a blond-haired boy around seven years old.

"Mister, you alright?"

"Yeah, I'm okay." I looked around for an adult that should have been with the boy. There was no one.

"Okay, just checking."

That short interaction encouraged me to continue.

Years later, a workmate gave me a white lab that was destined for the pound. Her name was Angel, and she looked a lot like that dog that licked my ear years ago. *Was that boy an angel? Can an angel look like a dog?*

Perhaps, at least for me.

Days after the dog/angel experience, I approached a middle-aged man for a donation at an outdoor street fair. "You're a Moonie! You should tell people that."

"Um...I'm wearing my Unification Church I.D. badge."

"Everyone doesn't know that's the Moonies. You're ashamed to tell them!"

"No, I'm not."

"Yes, you are!"

Suddenly I jumped up onto a picnic table and shouted, "Excuse me, everyone!" Around thirty people in the crowded plaza turned their heads toward me.

"This gentleman claims that I'm ashamed to tell people I'm a Moonie. Please know that I am indeed a Moonie and rather proud of that."

The man's face turned red while he scurried off.

I read somewhere that to build up self-assurance in their sales staff, a successful marketing company in Japan required all their sales trainees to act like chickens while standing on Tokyo street corners. Fundraising as a Moonie was a good chicken-on-the-corner substitute.

Many years after my MFT years, I returned to my hometown and got a job for a short while as a service/sales technician for the 7Up Bottling company. My boss called me "king of the cold call" because of my willingness to go after new accounts.

"Piece of cake," I told him.

After all, none of those potential customers call me brain-washed, swear at me, call the police or chase me with busted beer bottles.

My time on MFT was indeed a million-dollar experience where my confidence grew, and I learned so many things about myself and others.

Words are hard to find that can truly convey that experience. But I'll try.

Chapter Thirty-Nine
The Fugitive

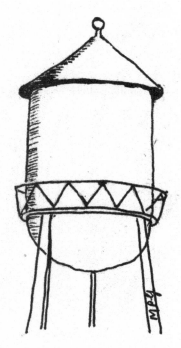

Who would have thought a water tower would create so much anxiety? But there it was, about five miles away. It wasn't one of those fancy towers, painted with a smiley face or the town's name, just a plain silver colored water tower. It was small, so the town ahead had to be small. Maybe a few thousand people.

It was mid-December in Wisconsin. A light dusting of snow shrouded fields of corn-stubble. The rising sun made a feeble attempt to break through the morning mist.

Will I find a place to store my extra product? Will the people be nice, or mean? Will I get arrested? Or beaten up?

At least it wasn't snowing. Or even worse, freezing rain.

I had just joined Patrick's fundraising team. He was a nice, capable guy. Tall and slender with blond hair, he looked Scandinavian, but with a name like Patrick, and the fact that he had once considered becoming a Catholic priest, suggested some Irish blood. He was also from California like me.

Please don't drop me off here, I prayed silently. There were two other people in the van, maybe he would pick them? My prayer wasn't answered.

"Bob, you're next. Here's a list of towns to hitchhike to if you finish with this one or get kicked out. Here's five bucks for food. Grab two boxes of candy from the back when I stop."

Apprehensively getting out with my boxes, I thought about finding a café to get a cup of coffee but knew that wasn't a good idea. I had to start fundraising. Plus, I didn't want to waste my money. Maybe I'd find some free coffee at a business. Hardware stores sometimes give away coffee to their customers. And feed stores.

First thing I needed to do was find some place to drop off my extra box, which weighed about ten pounds. Usually, a gas station might let me do that, but I had to be careful. They might be ill-disposed towards my church and steal it.

"What candy? We don't have your candy. You must be crazy."

I'd heard those words before. Thankfully, that seldom happened, but still...

"Sir, would you mind if I store this box of candy here? I'm fundraising for my church, and I'll be back later," I asked the man at the service station.

"Sure, no problem. I'm usually gone for lunch though, and I close at six. Just stick it in the corner."

I was glad that was over. It could be a real pain finding somewhere to store product. Probably wouldn't need that extra box anyway.

It was Saturday so I started going house to house. No one was donating, until finally:

"Come inside out of the cold, young man. How much did you say that candy was?" the middle-aged lady asked.

"One for two or three for five."

"Okay, I'll take three. I'll get my wallet and be right back."

As she left the room, a voice on a police scanner on the counter screeched,

"I don't see him anywhere. Where'd you say he's s'posed to be?"

"Myrtle over on Pioneer phoned it in about ten minutes ago."

"What's he look like?"

"She said stocky and under six feet tall. Wearin' one of them dark blue winter caps like you wear. Plus, he's carrying a cardboard box."

"I'm on Pioneer right now and there's no sign of him."

"I'll bet he's inside someone's house. Drive to the end of the street then down again. We'll catch that Moonie!"

Oh no, they're looking for me! Cautiously I looked out the window just as a police car drove by.

I started humming loudly to drown out the radio. Luckily, the conversation seemed to be over.

"What was all that commotion on the scanner?" the lady reappeared with her wallet. "Haven't heard that much activity since the Piggly Wiggly got fresh-made donuts. Not much happens around here."

I didn't answer her question as I quickly gave her three chocolate bars for her five dollars.

"Is there a mobile home park nearby?"

"Yes. It's at the southern end of town. About a fifteen-minute walk from here."

"Thanks for the donation. Enjoy your chocolates."

Watchfully exiting the front door, in the distance I could see the police cruiser slowly driving away. I dashed across an empty lot to a street behind the lady's house and hid behind a tree. *Good. No cars.* I continued running down side streets then through a large park where I found a plastic shopping bag for my chocolates and cap and threw away the cardboard box.

He'll never find me now. Good thing I heard that scanner.

Sheesh, you'd think I was an escaped convict instead of a church missionary.

As expected, the trailer park wasn't very big. Maybe twenty homes. At least they wouldn't be calling the police. Trailer park folks seldom did that.

I went trailer to trailer, knocking on doors. One young man asked me inside for a cup of coffee.

There's that free coffee I was hoping for.

"Take a seat on the couch. Cream and sugar?"

"One each please."

After a few minutes he placed a steaming cup on the coffee table. An open *Spiderman* comic book caught my attention. I glanced at it and felt upset by what I saw.

What's this? Reverend Egg Foo Yung is holding people hostage at Yankee Bean Stadium? It was an obvious satire of Reverend Moon and his 1976 *God Bless America Rally.* So stupid and infantile.

I can't believe it! Even comic books persecute us. Thankfully some people are nice, like this guy.

Savoring the hot beverage, I thought about the Bible verse where Jesus says whoever gives one of these little ones even a cup of cold water because he is a disciple, shall not lose his reward.

I imagined that cups of coffee count too.

"Would you like to watch some cartoons?"

"Sure, at least until I'm finished."

Tom and Jerry was on.

It had been a long time, maybe ten years, since I watched Saturday morning cartoons and I was mesmerized. However, not mesmerized enough to stay awake.

"Excuse me." I felt a nudge on my shoulder. "Hate to wake you. You're welcome to stay longer if you'd like. Thought you might want to be out selling your candy."

"How long was I sleeping?"

"Not too long. Maybe ten minutes. By the way, how much is your candy?"

"One for two. Three for five."

"I don't have much money but here's two bucks."

"Thank you for that. And the coffee. And the cartoons. And the nap. God bless you."

Handing him a strawberry-filled chocolate bar I stepped outside.

Dogs barked nearby as I continued knocking on trailer doors. Nearly everyone gave something, including some Mexican families who probably worked at a nearby dairy. Finally, I walked up to the trailer I always saved for last, the one marked Manager.

An older bearded man answered the door. "You can't sell those here. This is private property."

"Okay. Thanks for letting me know."

Chapter Forty
The Fugitive, continued

I left the trailer park and started walking along a railroad track. Far away I could see a grain silo and a train backing up to a line of grain cars. I ran up to the locomotive and climbed on board when it stopped. The engineer didn't notice me.

"Excuse me sir."

"What the hell...you're not supposed to be here! 'Bout crapped my pants. What can I do for you?"

"I'm asking donations for our church work. Would you like some chocolate bars?"

"How much?"

"One for two, three for five."

"Okay. I need a snack anyways. Give me three. Here's five dollars. Now get the hell out of here before we both get in trouble!"

Jumping from the train I ran to the grain mill and walked inside. It appeared deserted, but I explored the eerily quiet building hoping to find someone.

Peering into a small room I saw a card table surrounded by four rickety chairs. In front of each one, the table's reddish veneer was worn through to the wood underneath, where card-holding hands would rest. Small valleys had been created by years of card playing. As expected, a pot of warm coffee sat on a nearby counter.

I thought about grabbing another free cup but decided to find something for lunch downtown.

As I headed toward the front door, I heard a vehicle approaching and peeked out the window.

The police!

I started running through the mill along a path in the corn dust on the concrete floor with no idea where it led. Just as I heard the front door squeaking open behind me, footsteps echoed from the steel ceiling. In front of me a conveyor belt manlift began moving.

Maybe it's somebody that was taking a nap like my coworker used to do at the East Nicolaus rice dryer. I ran past the lift and followed the path out a side door. All right! The grain cars are still here! As I scurried onto a platform behind a grain hopper, the train began to move.

Wow! good timing. Seconds later I wouldn't have been able to escape onto the train. It would have been neat to ride it to its destination, but I had no idea where that was. Plus, there were chocolates at the service station. I'd have to jump off soon. I climbed onto a steel ladder and watched the ground move below me. Minutes later, when we were almost downtown, I leapt off and ran alongside the train while still holding onto the ladder, then let go.

That was fun. I'd always wanted to try hopping a train.

After the cars lumbered by, I walked across the tracks and noticed a John Deere cap lying in the gravel. It looked new. I picked it up, adjusted the headband to the largest size to fit my big head, then put it on. Now people will think I'm from around here.

It was about time for lunch.

Hmm, what'll it be? Cold chicken hot dogs from the Piggly Wiggly?

But then I'd have to eat outside, and it was cold. The hamburger joint across the street was closed for the winter. Soon I discovered Coffee Cup Café and went inside. It wasn't too busy: farmers at a table drinking coffee, a family with two young children, two old men at the counter. I took a seat near the old men and ordered the cheapest things on the menu: a bowl of chili, a grilled-cheese sandwich and a glass of water.

As I ate, farm commodity prices played on the radio. "Pork belly's sure down this year," a farmer muttered.

Suddenly a uniformed police officer walked in with a young man wearing a seed cap. I nervously gulped down the last bite of my sandwich.

He must have been at the mill to pick up that kid. The young man sat down while the officer walked toward the bathroom. I hastily paid my bill and left.

Man, this is crazy. Everywhere I go that cop shows up. It seemed like a sign that I should leave. But first I needed to write a note for Patrick.

I walked briskly to the post office, took a piece of paper out of a wastebasket and wrote: Heading North to next town. Current time: 12:35pm.

I folded it, found a small rock, then got on my knees to place the piece of paper underneath the large blue steel mailbox, with the rock holding it in place. What's this? I noticed another piece of paper under a rock next to a metal leg. It was also a note. I could barely read the faded writing. Kicked out of town. Heading north. I wondered who that was.

As I placed my note, I imagined another fundraiser might find it in the future.

The service station was closed. A handwritten Back at One sign hung in the window. As I looked at my watch, an old pickup pulled in and drove over the black hose lying across the driveway. Ding! A loud bell rang from inside the service station.

"Fill 'er up!" a gruff voice cried out.

"Um, I don't work here. The owner should be here in a few minutes. While you wait, you could snack on some delicious chocolate. By the way, are you heading north? I'm going to the next town."

The man looked confused as he stared at me and my Unification Church ID. His eyes widened. I noticed a small cross dangling from the rear-view mirror. He grabbed a booklet from the glove compartment and handed it to me. It was a Bible tract. I'd been offered hundreds of them, but this was the first one with a witch on the cover and the title, Bewitched?

I would add this to my collection.

"Read that and you'll know how to accept Jesus as your personal Savior."

"If you're heading north to the next town, I could read it while you're driving."

"I can give you a ride to the station on the highway. You'll have better luck there. So, have you ever accepted Jesus as your personal savior?"

Hundreds of times, I wanted to tell him, but didn't want to get into it. Thankfully, the garage owner was back.

"Need 'er filled up, Jack?"

"Yep. Just put it on my bill."

Soon Farmer Jack and I were heading down the road with my chocolates bouncing around on my lap. As the cross swung back and forth from the rear-view mirror, I studied the Bewitched tract as promised. While doing so I recollected one of our church songs, Suffering Jesus, which had inspired me to pray to Jesus to help me understand his heart...something I almost regretted when I walked into a large night club in Northern Wisconsin with a case of brandy snifters filled with wax and made into candles. I asked some of the patrons if they would be interested in purchasing my fine product.

"It's a Moonie! It's a Moonie!" a man in the crowd of about thirty people yelled.

Somebody tried to yank the box of candles from me. The box ripped and brandy glasses crashed to the floor. A couple of burley guys grabbed hold of me and started parading me around the night club as people spat and poured their beer on me. That's when I remembered praying to know the heart of Jesus. Lord, forgive them, for they know not what they do. I felt no animosity or hatred toward those people. However, I told Jesus that was about all I could handle after I was thrown out the door and onto the ground. The owner of the night club kicked me and stomped on what was left of my candles.

Soon we stopped at the highway station and Jack said, "I'd like to say a prayer before you leave."

I bowed my head.

"Dear Lord, please guide this young man. I pray he can see the dark web of deception he is caught up in and accept you as his personal savior. In the name of Jesus, Amen."

"Uh, thank you for that...and the ride."

After I got out, Jack popped the clutch on the rusted truck. The rear wheels spun slightly in the snow and gravel then moved forward.

I placed my box and bag of chocolates against the building where I could see them while soliciting another ride.

"Excuse me ma'am. I'm a church missionary and I'm trying to catch a ride to the next town," I asked a middle-aged woman who was hanging up a gas nozzle.

She peered at my ID, then gasped and bolted into her car and locked the door. Her children locked theirs.

Shaking my head, I walked back to my chocolates to await my next prospect.

Within minutes a green Buick pulled up to the gas pumps. A slender woman in a green beret and long, flowery dress got out and walked into the store then back to the gas pumps. She looked about thirty. As she was putting gas into her car, I walked up and gave her my spiel. She glanced at my ID, smiled, hung up the nozzle, then said, "Sure, I'll give you a ride. You were at my aunt's house earlier and she bought some candy. Apparently, the cops were looking for you. She heard it on her scanner."

"Does she want her money back?"

"Heck no," she chuckled. "She thinks it's funny how her neighbors are in a kerfuffle because you're in town. She's always supporting the underdog. But we should get going. Officer Fred might be hot on your tail."

Seated in the passenger's seat with my product on my lap, I stared at the crystals hanging from the rearview mirror as my hippie chauffeur drove away.

"My name's Suzie. And you are?"

"Bob."

"Nice to meet you, Bob. I've never met a chocolate-selling criminal before..."

"Oh," Suzie exclaimed as she glanced into the rear-view mirror. "Don't turn around. In fact, you might want to hunch down a bit. Looks like Officer Fred's pulling into the gas station right now...hope I don't get busted for harboring a fugitive!"

Chapter Forty-One
Night Sounds

"Snowy Night" Marion Wilcott Photographer
Farm Security Administration public domain

It was a cold night at the beginning of 1979. Really cold, not just for this California boy, but even for Wisconsin natives.

As I plodded downhill on a Racine sidewalk toward Lake Michigan, I could hear a faint jingle far away. It sounded like sleigh bells. Santa's sleigh bells. But that couldn't be, it was January. Santa was probably back in the North Pole or taking a much-deserved vacation in the Bahamas.

As the jingling became louder, I realized what it was: Tim running up the street toward me, coins rattling in his pockets. He and I had been dropped off at opposite ends of a strip of bars and nightclubs and were working our way toward each other.

Suddenly it stopped. He must be going inside a bar.

I wanted to keep moving toward him, but I was tired.

A few yards ahead I could see steam rising from a sewer. I trudged over to the grate and sat down on the curb next to it. It was smelly, and a little warmer, but not much. The steam quickly fogged my glasses. I closed my eyes and thought of California. I was homesick.

My dad would make bonfires this time of year, with wood scraps from the survey stakes he used to make as a side business. I'd stand near the fire and drink hot chocolate, listening to migrations of birds flying overhead. They sounded so close. I used to look up, hoping the fire might illuminate the waterfowl, but the Sacramento Valley fog was way too thick.

There would be other night sounds. A plane flying to, or away from, Beale Air Force Base. A car traveling on Beale Road a half mile away. My parents arguing inside the house. A cow mooing in the distance.

Night sounds were so different here in Racine. Loose tire chains flapping. Snow shovels scraping sidewalks. Snow blowers blowing. Ships on the lake sounding their horns, talking to each other in a language only mariners understand. A freight train accelerating while moving forward, loud clangs filling the night as each car jerks out of its slumber. Coins clinking inside pockets.

Tim didn't last long inside that bar. He'd be here soon; he was always running. I got up to head toward him.

Tim was a Communist before joining the church. A real Communist who practiced what he preached, not one of those counterfeit Commies I'd encountered in college towns like Madison, with their black berets and Che Guevara T-shirts.

He told me how he'd ride his bicycle through the snow in Cleveland to hand out pamphlets to factory workers. He'd been beaten up a few times.

We were a motley crew of church fundraisers: me, the formerly bearded, long-haired vegetarian hippie from a small town in Northern California; Commie Tim from Cleveland; Lowell, once a pig farmer from Minnesota who used to drink too much; and our team leader, Patrick, who had aspired to the Catholic priesthood. Patrick was from Southern California and his dad was a college professor.

Tim and I had almost met up. In addition to the jangling coins, the buckles on his snow-boots made a clicking sound as he ran toward me.

"Where...where...we goin' next?" he panted as he ran up to me.

"Don't know about you, but I'm going to a McDonalds or some place to warm up and get somethin' to eat. You're from Cleveland, you're used to this weather."

"There's a café about five blocks down the street. They were negative and kicked me out. Guess they can't stop us from eating there."

"Hopefully they won't spit in our food."

"We can sit at the counter and keep an eye on the cook."

"Sounds like a plan," I said.

"Let's go." Tim started running.

"Wait a second! You can run there if you so desire. I'm walking. Order me a bowl o' chili, a grilled cheese sandwich and a coffee. I'll pay you when I get there."

"Okay!"

As he ran out of sight, I could still hear the jingling of his coins and the clanging of his boot buckles. Maybe someone else would hear him, perhaps a child, and think it was Santa's sleigh.

But that would be silly. It was January.

Chapter Forty-Two

Moonie on the Block!

"**Betty**, call the shopkeepers and townspeople. Warn them there's a Moonie in town," was the response when I asked the hardware store owner in a small northern Wisconsin town if he would like to give a donation for a butterfly pin to help our church.

"Come here, young man, I've got something to show you!" he said proudly as I followed him into his office. "Look!"

On the main wall, instead of the usual hardware office decor of mounted stuffed fish, deer heads, and calendars of scantily clad women hawking pipe wrenches, were hundreds of sensational articles about the Unification Church.

Wow, this guy needs a life.

"What do you think?"

I wanted to tell him, "I think you're a religious bigot!" but held my tongue. From glancing at a few articles, I could guess that I'd already read most of them. My aunt from Duluth kept my parents informed about how terrible my church was by clipping derogatory articles and mailing them to California. My mother would then religiously send them to me.

Wishing him a good day, I walked outside and looked down the street. *This is going to be an interesting day.*

Visiting other businesses proved futile since every shopkeeper had been warned about me. Finishing the commercial area in record time (having someone yell "no" at you when you open the door doesn't take long), I started to go house to house. Although many of the residents had been alerted, I was still able to gain some success. However, it was soon to become more difficult.

One gentleman, perhaps a relative of the hardware store owner, apparently believed it was his personal responsibility to follow me to every house to inform residents I was brainwashed and worked for a cult. Luckily, I was able to outrun my overweight middle-aged stalker, and knock on a few doors without his presence. However, he started following me in his car and whenever a potential customer opened their door, he'd blare on the horn and shake his head vigorously. Sadly, this harassment technique worked. No one was donating.

I've got to get away from this blockhead.

Sprinting down a side street and into a driveway, I hid behind an old pickup truck. The guy drove past, and I jogged toward downtown. As I ran past a small run-down gas station where I'd been earlier, a frail elderly lady motioned for me to come inside.

"What's all the commotion about? You seem like a nice young man. People here are so mean. I'm sorry I didn't buy anything earlier. Show me those butterfly pins. I'd like to pick something for my granddaughters."

As she looked at the pins, I glanced out a dingy cracked window and saw a car drive by. It was my persecutor and he looked frustrated.

"They're two for five dollars, right?"

"Yes."

"I'll take two."

When she handed me a five-dollar bill with a quivering hand I almost cried. "Thank you so much. You've made my day."

I ran back to knock on doors in the neighborhood I'd just left. Now that I'd shaken off that clown maybe I'd have some success.

Unfortunately, my reprieve only lasted about ten minutes.

"Moonie on the block! Red alert! Moonie on the block!"

My middle-aged tormentor was replaced by a group of six kids on bicycles. They also followed me to front doors to yell their warnings. One of the miscreants pelted me with pebbles.

Their plan backfired. People must've felt sorry for me and started donating. One man even yelled at the juvenile delinquents to get the hell off his lawn. Soon the adolescent biker gang pedaled off to find a dog to kick or a mailbox to knock down.

Near the edge of town, I spotted a dirt road leading to a tiny house in the distance. I walked up to it. The humble cottage was well-maintained and beautiful flowers were growing everywhere. To the side was a flourishing vegetable garden. Chickens cackled unseen from a backyard.

As I knocked on the screen door, I could see an elderly couple seated at a table. They appeared to be reading something. Soon the lady came to the door. She was in a flowery dress.

"Please come in, we've been waiting for you."

Waiting for me? Did someone tell them I'd be stopping by? Or--?

"Please take a seat," she said, pulling out a chair at the small kitchen table on which two Bibles lay open. On another chair was an elderly man with a medium length white beard who nodded and smiled.

As I sat down, the woman poured me a glass of cold lemonade.

"Oatmeal or chocolate chip cookies?"

"Um, oatmeal please," I responded, dumbfounded.

After placing two cookies and a napkin in front of me, she sat down. "Now show me what you're selling."

I moved the box of butterfly pins closer to her and she studied them intently.

"Two for five dollars, right?"

"Uh, yeah..." I wondered how she knew.

"I'll take these two. Sam, give this young man five dollars."

He silently reached for his wallet, pulled out a five-dollar bill and handed it to me. A cuckoo clock cuckooed seven times. As I sipped lemonade and munched cookies, I looked around the room.

On a nearby wall hung family photos. Next to one of a young man was a glass-covered triangular box containing a folded American flag.

Through a window screen, I could hear birds singing and chickens cackling and felt like I was in an oasis, a refuge from all the hatred and misunderstanding of the world.

After my last sip of lemonade, I thanked the couple for their kindness and support and stood up. They both smiled and nodded. The gentleman stood up too and followed me to the door. As I exited, he said, "God bless you and be safe."

I walked back down the dirt road in a daze. When I reached the end, a police cruiser pulled up beside me.

"Young man," said the earnest young officer, "I know you have every right to do this, but I suggest you stop for the day. There's a town hall meeting taking place right now. People are angry and they want you out of here. No tellin' what they'll do."

"Okay. I'm about done anyway and I'm s'posed to be picked up at eight. I understand how Jesus must have felt getting kicked out of towns." What the policeman said next has stayed etched in my memory for decades, I was so stunned by his heartfelt response.

"Yeah, and I know what it must have been like for Pontius Pilate."

Wow. I felt so grateful. He could have harassed and arrested me, as many other policemen did, over the course of five years.

I walked to the post office where I was to be picked up. The streets were mostly deserted, and I guessed most of the town was at that meeting. Sitting down, I reflected about my day: about the elderly lady at the gas station, the policeman, the various people who gave donations while someone was screaming at them not to. In particular, I thought about the couple at the end of the dirt road who were reading their Bibles when I knocked on the door.

Around eight the fundraising van picked me up and I counted my donations. I had made exactly one hundred dollars, which was my goal for that time period. A sister asked me about my day. "Well, when I walked into a hardware store..."

Chapter Forty-Three
Butterflies 'n' Beer

"Whatcha sellin'?" a skinny, thirtyish man asks as I walk near his table inside the dingy, smoke-filled, working-class bar in rural Iowa during the summer of 1979. It's after 10pm but still warm and muggy.

"Butterfly pins."

"Butterfly pins?"

"Yes. They're hand painted Cloisonné enameled metal brooches."

"Lemme see. I might wanna get somethin' for my daughter."

Walking closer, I place the tray carrying a dozen pins neatly displayed in their individual boxes near my potential customer.

"Could you hold 'em closer? I can't see very well in this light."

"Uh, sure."

Moving the tray closer, I still hold onto it with one hand and wait uneasily for the man to decide, worried he might try to steal them. His two dust-covered friends sit ominously quiet as Patsy Cline's song, *I Fall to Pieces*, plays on the jukebox.

"You musta bin at the feed mill earlier today. I think the secketary bought one of those. Folks said you're sellin' for those Moonies. That right?" He glances at the Unification Church ID pinned to my shirt.

"Uh, yeah..."

"Hmm."

He slowly reaches for an empty Coors bottle and spits into it. A small drop of tobacco-laced spittle makes a path down his flour-covered chin, and I worry the spit might drip onto the butterflies. He then touches his sweat-stained DeKalb seed cap like he's a baseball coach sending a secret signal to one of his players.

Suddenly one of the overly quiet friends jumps from his seat, grabs my free arm, and twists it behind my back. My pretend customer then yanks his arm from underneath the table and pulls out a pre-shaken Coors bottle, lifts his thumb from the bottle top and sprays me and my tray of butterflies with a shower of beer.

"Get the hell outta my town and never come back!"

The bar roars with laughter.

As I calmly grab my beer-soaked tray of butterflies and walk toward the door, the last verse of Cline's song plays on the jukebox.

Further down the road I sit at a picnic table next to a closed ice cream parlor, eerily illuminated by the blue light of a bug zapper.

The zapper zaps continuously as it electrocutes its deceived victims. *Bzzzt. Bzzzt.* Faint smells of vaporized insects and beer-soaked clothing fill the night air.

My watch says 10:20. Patrick should be here with the van soon.

Pouring beer out of the cardboard tray and the small boxes, I wipe the butterflies with a dry area of my T-shirt, spreading everything out on the table. I then close my eyes and start humming *I Fall to Pieces*.

I knew the song well. Listened to it as a kid while hanging out with my dad at the Royal Oak Tavern in Linda. He also sang it around the house.

Just as I start to nod off, I'm wakened to the sound of glass breaking.

"Git 'im!"

It's my tormentors from the bar charging toward me with broken beer bottles!

Someone swings at me, but I duck, and he hits some of the brooches and drying boxes, scattering them to the ground. I jump up and run faster than I've ever run in my life. I'm not a fast runner, but at least I'm not drunk. Plus, at twenty-five, I'm probably ten years younger than these hayseeds. Luckily two of my attackers lose their breath and can't keep up, but the rube that held me in the bar is getting closer. I don't think I can outrun him, but I remember a dirty trick a base runner played on me back in high school when I was a catcher for the Marysville Indians baseball team.

You've gotta do this right. Don't panic. You can do this.

"I'm gonna kill you real good, you brainwashed Moonie!"

I dash across someone's front lawn aiming toward a rose bush. Seconds before he touches me, I fall to the ground and my pursuer trips over my body and flies into the thorny branches. Leaping up, I run back into the street just in time to escape the other yokels as they continue to run after me. A sound of agonized groaning comes from the rose bush.

If that guy gets up and catches me, he's really going to kill me.

Suddenly I hear a horn honking and a vehicle coming towards us. It's Patrick! The startled clodhoppers dive out of the way and Patrick drives the van next to me while I'm still running. The side door opens and someone yells, "Jump in!"

I dive, and a brother grabs me.

"That was close," Patrick exclaims. "You okay? What's that beer smell? What happened?"

"Tell you later. My butterflies are back at the ice cream parlor. Should we go get them?"

"Nah... are you nuts? Grab some more from the back of the van. There's another town about thirty-five minutes from here. I'll drop you off there."

Chapter Forty-Four

Pray For Me

Robert Armitage Sterndale, Public domain, via Wikimedia
Commons - 1886 {{PD-US-expired}}

"**W**ill you pray for me?" the elderly woman asked somberly as she grasped my hand.

"Of course, what would you like me to pray?"

"I'm afraid my family wants to stick me into an old folks' home. They think I can't take care of myself. I'd rather die than move into one of those horrid places."

I held her hands and we prayed as we stood together on the sidewalk near her apartment in the small retirement community.

It was amazing how someone would open their heart to me, a stranger hawking candy, flowers, or trinkets for my church. Usually, it was an elderly person who would look beyond the unfavorable media portrayal of me as a brainwashed member of the Unification Church and see me as a sincere young man who loved God and wanted to help people.

When Reverend Moon first came to America, he was saddened to see elderly people set aside and forgotten in nursing homes. He shared many stories of how wonderful it was to have his grandparents close by while he was growing up in a small village in North Korea. He taught that ideally, households should be made up of three generations.

Although my mother died before my children were born, my dad lived nearby for the last twenty years of his life. For most of his final years he lived in a nice trailer on our property. It was often difficult taking care of him, but I believe my family benefited from his presence.

One of my favorite places to go when I was fundraising was apartments above shops in the downtown area of towns and cities.

"You're the only person that's knocked on my door in over a year," the startled elderly woman told me as I stood outside her apartment above a business in a small city in Iowa.

She invited me inside and asked if I would like some lemonade. When I said yes, she also brought me cookies and shared with me how much she missed her family who had left Iowa. I didn't say much, just munched and listened as she talked about her life. I wasn't in that tidy, memento-filled apartment long and can't remember all the stories she shared, but I still remember her kindness. I'm quite sure, although it took minimal effort on my part, that I also brought some joy to that little old lady at the top of a quiet staircase.

Sometimes I could spend weeks never hearing a kind word or shred of encouragement from the people I approached, so when it did happen it was immensely memorable.

It was late one evening when I walked up to an elderly gentleman filling up his tank at a gas station and asked if he could give a ride to a couple of church missionaries, me and my friend Tom, to the next small mid-western town. He said he'd love to and soon we were heading down the highway with this kind man and his wife.

We hadn't gone far when suddenly the siren and flashing red lights of a police cruiser were behind us. Our startled driver pulled over and stopped the car. A police officer walked up to the driver's window.

"Don't worry, we're just after those boys in back."

"What'd they do? Aren't they missionaries?"

"No, they're not, they're cultists and we don't want them in our town."

"But... they're *leaving* your town!" the Good Samaritan countered as a deputy asked Tom and me to get out of the car.

The officer, whose "uniform" consisted of blue jeans and the word POLICE spelled in glitter across his T-shirt, patted us hardened criminals down and handcuffed us. To my surprise our driver hung around. He was told he could leave, but instead he got out and said, "I can still give you guys a ride if you need it."

"Thanks for the offer," I replied, "but it looks like we'll be spending the night in the crossbar hotel. You're a good man! God bless you."

One of my favorite stories that still causes me to chuckle is about a decrepit old man in a wheelchair at a nursing home.

While traveling on my own throughout the Midwest selling pictures and living out of a van, I would often make my best sales at nursing homes because the pictures, which had no glass, were lightweight, safe, and durable. Often employees at the facilities would also buy.

At one of those homes, I set up pictures in the lobby and many people were admiring them, especially the one of a Siberian Tiger. As my potential customers started to comment and ooh and ah about the tiger, an old man who could barely sit up on his own and looked as if he didn't have much longer to live, cried out in his crackly voice, "Tiger? Why is everyone talking about me?"

I've met them all: cranky and mean senior citizens as well as nice, kind, and caring ones.

My dad was a hybrid. Often cranky, but also kind and caring. For over twenty years he owned the Wheatland Fruit Stand. He'd give free flowers to people visiting the local cemetery, candy to kids, special deals to customers with large families and he often helped stranded motorists. He saved his anger mostly for wholesalers who tried to cheat him, the Yuba County Health Department, and the "Fruit Police" (agricultural inspectors enforcing California's stone fruit marketing order).

When I'm old, I want to be like that "tiger" at the old folks' home, bringing some joy to an often-sad world.

Chapter Forty-Five
Shoeless Bob

A bitterly cold, howling wind that blew snow around the reservation also carried sounds of laughter and car doors slamming from the small group of ramshackle houses about a quarter of a mile away. The faint sounds reached my crimson-red ears.

Three white cars approached me on the gravel road: two Chevy Impalas, the most common car on the reservation, and a Ford Fairlane.

I'll bet they're all missing the back seat.

It was mid-December in North Dakota, and I was freezing.

I was missing a shoe, and my ripped pants leg flapped uncontrollably behind me as I tried to stay warm by jogging in place. I stuck out like a partly naked red-haired white guy jumping around on a dirt road on an isolated Indian Reservation.

Two of the cars slowed down as adults in the front seat and children in the back pointed and laughed at my predicament. The Fairlane pulled up next to me and a back window rolled down.

"Here's your shoe, man," a teenaged male smirked. "See, we're honest injuns."

"Gee thanks!" I smiled back, noticing the back seat had been replaced by a mattress.

"You gonna be okay?" shouted the driver from the front seat.

"Yeah, I'll be okay. Someone's picking me up soon. Thanks for asking."

"You're welcome. Thanks for giving us a good laugh."

As he turned the car around, the teenager and a bunch of laughing kids stared at me through the back window while I put on my tattered soaking wet Kmart tennis shoe. Tennis shoes were good for fundraising; you could easily run in them, and they were warm enough if you wore wool socks. In really wet weather you could slip galoshes over them.

I had been going door-to-door selling and trading turquoise jewelry on a reservation.

After running up some wooden steps to a house, I knocked on the door. As I waited, I could hear the faint rattle of a chain below me.

Uh-oh.

Sure enough, connected to that chain was a medium-sized black and white dog that bolted around and up the steps after me. When I held out my foot to protect myself it chomped onto my shoe, shook its head from side to side and growled ferociously. Suddenly, it yanked off my shoe. As I made a feeble run for it, the angry mutt bit into my pants leg. As it growled and tugged at my light blue corduroys, I dragged the animal across the snow-covered dirt yard until we reached the end of the chain.

We were in a man versus dog tug-of-war.

I pulled and pulled but the mongrel wouldn't let go. Then suddenly my pants leg ripped, from the ankle all the way up to the waistband. The dog had torn off a wide strip of fabric from the outer seam area, enabling me to escape its wrath.

At last I was safe. Freezing, but safe. I looked at my watch. Thankfully, Danny would be here soon.

I hobbled to our rendezvous point along the dirt road to wait, and unintentionally provided entertainment for some of the locals.

On the reservations we'd trade for handcrafts, fireworks and sometimes food. One of my most memorable trades happened on Red Lake Indian Reservation in Minnesota.

"I wish I could afford more of your jewelry," the woman said after purchasing some earrings. "I've got too many grandchildren."

"I'll trade you for a couple of dinners for me and my partner. We haven't had a home cooked meal in a long time and whatever you're cooking sure smells good."

"That's venison. My grandsons shoot deer." She opened the door to the garage and revealed two skinned carcasses hanging from the rafters. "I'd love to trade. What are you offering?"

"How about twenty dollars' worth of jewelry for two home cooked meals?"

"Sounds good to me."

"Okay. I'll go find my partner and we'll be back in about an hour."

When we returned, I was shocked by the feast awaiting us: venison steaks, wild rice from nearby rivers and lakes, fish from Red Lake, wild blueberries, and fry bread with home-canned chokecherry jam.

As we ate, our hosts started speaking in Chippewa while examining jewelry, and a cassette player filled the small room with Native American music.

"It doesn't get much better than this," I told Danny. "It's like we're back in the olden days trading trinkets to the Indians. But I think they're getting a better deal this time around."

"We'd better be," a middle-aged woman chuckled. "If not, we might have to scalp you. I've been eyeing that red hair of yours."

"Uh, how 'bout we make that thirty dollars' worth of jewelry. I didn't expect this much food."

I glanced at Danny. He nodded in approval.

"Wahkay Alloway, Wahkay Alloway..."

The young man beat his drum as he tried to teach me the words of a Native American song about horses dancing. As I listened, his wife continued to string beads together so she could finish the *Divine Principle* beaded book cover I ordered.

I had met the couple after knocking on their door about a year earlier. While they were looking at the jewelry I was selling, I noticed handmade beadwork throughout their house.

"Who did all the beadwork?"

"I did," replied the woman.

"It's beautiful. Would you like to trade for some jewelry?"

She picked out several turquoise necklace and earring sets. I found some beaded belt buckles and several necklaces I liked, and we traded.

We continued our business relationship, and I began sending her drawings of designs for her to make. I was back on the North Dakota reservation to pick up the pieces I had ordered, including the book cover.

As I continued to practice my Native American singing, my voice coach stopped for a moment.

"I'd like to give you something," he said as he stopped beating his drum, then walked into a bedroom. He came back with a decorated five-foot long shaft and handed it to me.

"This is a gift in honor of our friendship. It's wrapped with deer hide. That's an eagle's claw on the end. On the other end is a carved deer antler. I carved the antler, and my wife did the beadwork. The feathers hanging from the shaft are real eagle feathers."

"Wow. Thank you." I was speechless.

As I thought about what to say, his wife brought me the beaded book cover.

"All done."

"Wow, that's amazing! Thank you for everything. Especially the friendship staff, I'll cherish it. This has been an incredible afternoon."

When I got to my car and looked over the book cover, I realized this couple had never asked me about my church. I also realized that of all the years I'd been fundraising on Indian reservations I had never been called names or otherwise persecuted for my religion by a Native American.

However, one time I was persecuted for being a white guy by members of the American Indian Movement (AIM). One day at a powwow, after such mistreatment, I asked a wrinkled elderly gentleman in a chiefly looking costume what he thought of AIM. The man paused thoughtfully as I patiently waited to hear his insights. To this day I have never forgotten the reply.

"You mean, Assholes In Moccasins?"

Meeting the Indigenous People of America was a deep experience for me. I loved their kindness, wisdom, and open heart. I also sensed their suffering and felt sorry for it.

As I began my drive toward Minneapolis, I popped in a cassette tape of music I acquired at a powwow. Recognizing one of the songs, I sang along.

"Wahkay Alloway, Wahkay Alloway..."

Chapter Forty-Six

Crossbar Hotels

"God bless America!"

The irony was as thick as the packed Minnesota snow outside the jailhouse. The words and melody of the classic song filled the stark room and echoed off the concrete walls as Danny and I sang out and Native Americans from the drunk tank joined in.

Just as we got to the part about oceans white with foam, a metal door unlatched and eerily squeaked open as a middle-aged woman in a jailer's uniform stepped inside and walked over to me.

"You boys responsible for this?" she asked as I stopped singing and sheepishly nodded.

She looked down the hallway and then back at me. I heard sadness in her voice as she replied, gently shaking her head.

"You boys don't belong here."

Danny continued energetically singing as the jailer stood and listened until we got to the final lines of the patriotic song. Danny repeated the last line, and I joined in.

A loud clang rang out, cymbal-like, when the jailer shut the metal door just as the song ended.

Maybe Danny just liked the acoustics of a jail cell, because he was always singing every time we got arrested. One time he stood up on a stainless-steel commode and started belting out Frank Sinatra songs. I wanted him to stop because I needed a nap. However, it looked like our fellow inmates were enjoying his singing and I did not want to get on their bad side.

Danny and I, along with many other Unification Church members, spent a lot of time enjoying the amenities of America's so-called crossbar hotels because so many people were not happy that we were out raising funds for our controversial church.

If I had more carefully documented the range of experiences we had in the various locations where we were housed and fed courtesy of America's taxpayers, I might be able to publish some type of handbook about midwestern police departments and the quality of their lodgings. Sort of like a *Michelin Guide to America's Jailhouses*, with ratings for tightness of handcuffs, pleasantness (or otherwise) of the ride in the police car, quality of food, friendliness of staff and customers, and the ambience of the jail cell.

It seemed that many jails were designed by the same company. For the most part, if you've seen one, you've seen 'em all. However, one thing that separates a mediocre forced vacation from a great one is the quality of the staff. My vote for my best jailhouse experience goes to Ogden, Utah.

(Now please do not travel to Ogden and get arrested just because of my recommendation. That was a long time ago, and things might have changed.)

In Ogden my arrest had nothing to do with religious bigotry. The police had already warned me that if I continued to peddle my wares, especially on a Sunday in Utah, I would be arrested. When I explained the situation to my new team leader, he told me that if I kept the right attitude, the spirit world would protect me, and everything would be fine.

Well, I guess my attitude was lousy, because after knocking on just a few doors, Ogden's boys-in-blue were taking me for a ride.

"Why didn't you stop selling when we told you to?" one of the officers asked.

Although they were probably Mormons, I doubted they would sympathize with my "spirit world should've protected me" defense and simply told them my team leader made me do it.

One of the reasons Ogden was a good place for incarceration was that they didn't have many customers to deal with and could be more attentive to their guests. When I was locked up, there were only two of us there: me and a wayward teenager who'd been busted for stealing a car. The place was super clean, and the staff was friendly. They fed us McDonald's for dinner and breakfast.

Except for Ogden, I was always jailed because I was raising funds for the "Moonies." Interestingly those arrests, which may have been over fifty, never showed up as a record. We were never officially charged with anything, as far as I could tell. We seldom spent the night in a jail-cell and when we did, we always got bailed out the next morning.

However, I worked with an African American brother who was attacked by a hammer-wielding white man. To defend himself he hit the attacker and was arrested for assault. He spent several months in a county jail.

Years later I was able to receive a Secret security clearance (just one level below Top Secret) to work on military bases.

"Wow, Bob. You must be a saint or lead a really boring life because you got one of the fastest clearances I've ever seen," the security officer told me when I was working in the maintenance department of a military installation on Shemya Island, Alaska, many years later.

Unfortunately, our founder had a much rougher course in America. In the 1980s, when he was in his 60s, he was unfairly charged with criminal tax fraud, convicted by a jury, and served 13 months of a 15-month sentence at a minimum-security prison in Danbury, Connecticut. Christian leaders as politically diverse as Tim La Haye and Joseph Lowery spoke out against the verdict and pledged to spend a week in jail with Rev Moon. He was released early because of good behavior.

Never one to complain, Rev Moon told the members that Danbury was "not prison, more like country club." And he would know, having endured, in his earlier years, both the North and South Korean versions of incarceration as well as torture by the Imperial Japanese (as a student member of the Korean independence movement). He survived more than three years in a communist labor camp. If anyone could write a handbook it would be him.

One Pulitzer Prize winning author Carlton Sherwood investigated the tax case and wrote a book entitled Inquisition: The Persecution and Prosecution of the Reverend Sun Myung Moon. Though hefty looking and dealing with a complex topic, the book is extremely readable and hard to put down. I highly recommend it.

Chapter Forty-Seven
Danny Boy

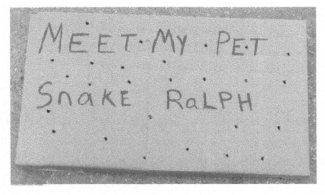

Danny and I were a two-man team of fundraisers traveling throughout the Midwest selling jewelry. We went everywhere: Indian reservations, cargo ships on the Great Lakes, factories, rodeos, county fairs, house-to-house, bars, strip joints, small towns, big towns, powwows, trains, and river barges.

We slept inside our bright yellow Pinto station wagon, on park benches or college dorm couches and occasionally, in a motel when Danny or I traded a room for some jewelry.

We were good at bartering. Especially Danny.

Danny was a punk living on the streets of San Francisco when he joined the Unification Church. He had at least a dozen piercings: ears, nose, lips, and who knows where else. He would often fill up some piercings with jewelry and tie a bandanna around his head before driving up to the window of a fast-food restaurant.

"May I help you?" the young lady asked in a surprised voice because we hadn't ordered anything from the order station before driving up.

"Why yes, my dear lassie. We're wayfarin' strangers travelin' through your village, and we'd love tradin' some o' this fine jewelry for some vittles and perhaps a couple root beers," Danny proclaimed in his best pirate voice as he held out a velvet covered board filled with cheap costume jewelry.

Surprisingly the young lady, who was the manager, played along.

"Why yes, I see you have some fine jewelry. I could possibly trade a couple hamburgers, fries and some root beers for something."

"How's about this exquisite emerald necklace with matchin' earrings? Formerly worn by an African queen she was."

"Why yes. That would be a good trade indeed. Your meals will be ready in just a few minutes."

I was cracking up and so were some of the restaurant staff. Two meals for fifty cents worth of jewelry. Not bad.

I first met Danny when he joined our fundraising team in the Midwest. He was so unlike me. He was from a large city on the East Coast, his parents were upper middle class, he'd attended private Catholic schools and was very extroverted.

Sadly, he hated his parents and wouldn't share why. Members of the team would encourage him to write to them and pray for reconciliation.

He was always doing silly things. One day, we were working a mostly African American neighborhood together; I believe it was in Chicago. We were selling silk roses in a business area. Our plan was for Danny to go east down the street for five blocks, cross the street and then head west. I would do the opposite and we would keep working until we ran into each other. After a couple of hours, I caught up with him and was shocked at what I saw.

He was in a pool hall where it looked like a couple of young Black men were ready to pummel him with their pool cues, except it soon became clear that it wasn't him they wanted to attack. It was his cardboard box. Normal fundraisers on the team simply carried their silk roses in a large bouquet as they solicited donations. But not Danny. He had taken a cardboard rose shipping box and poked holes in it with a pen. Next to the holes, he had written with a Sharpie:

Meet my pet snake Ralph.

Meeting Ralph was of no interest to these men.

"Don't you dare open that box! We don't wanna see no goddam snake! Get the hell outta here!"

He ignored their pleas and opened the box, laughing.

"Just kidding. It's fake flowers. I'm fundraising for my church."

Unfortunately, no one else was laughing and I thought *now* they might pummel him with their pool sticks.

"Danny!" I shouted. "Let's get out of here. Sorry 'bout that guys. He didn't mean any harm."

They lowered their potential weapons and shook their heads as we quickly left.

One evening we were going door to door at apartments where you use an intercom to ask occupants to buzz you in. Danny randomly pushed a button.

"Yes. May I help you?"

"It's Dan. Could you buzz me in?"

"Dan? I don't know a Dan."

"Oh sorry. Wrong button."

"Hmm. Let's try this couple. Couples are good. They might think I'm the other person's friend."

He pushed the button. Within seconds there was a *Bzzt,* without anyone asking who it was, and I opened the door.

"Great! That was easy. I'll start at the top floor, and you start at the bottom, and we'll work toward each other. Good luck!"

After around half an hour of soliciting, I knocked on an apartment door and much to my surprise, Danny answered!

"Come on in. We've been waiting for you. I told this nice lady you'd have a different selection of jewelry from me. She wants to see what you've got."

"Okay." I walked inside and placed my jewelry display on a coffee table in front of the middle-aged woman.

After a few minutes there was another knock at the door and Danny answered it again.

"Who was that?" the lady asked.

"Oh, just some fella telling me to keep an eye out for some guys selling jewelry. I'm supposed to call security if I see anyone."

"Uh...that's you!"

"Probably so...unless there's someone else selling too. Should I call security?"

"No, that would be silly. Besides, I want to buy something."

When I meet Mormons, I often tell them I spent time in jail in Keokuk, Iowa, across the Mississippi River from where Joseph Smith, founder of the Mormon church, was murdered.

Danny and I were both arrested in Keokuk for selling jewelry door to door, once it was discovered we were with the Unification Church.

"We only have enough money to bail out one person. How 'bout I get out, make some money and come back to get you?" Danny wondered inside our jail cell.

"Sounds like a plan. But don't get arrested!"

Within hours, Danny was back with the money to set me free.

"Wow. How'd you do so well? You must've made hundreds of dollars."

"I drove around to bars and told customers I was selling jewelry to raise bail for my friend. They'd ask what he was in jail for. I'd tell them, selling without a permit. Then they'd laugh and usually buy or donate."

It was Danny who was with me in that memorable St. Paul jail cell. It was him belting out Frank Sinatra songs and *God Bless America* while standing on a stainless-steel commode.

One day, Danny left to visit his parents on the East coast. It was the last time I ever saw him. His parents had him kidnapped and "deprogrammed."

Years later, miraculously, a church sister we both knew ran into Danny in San Francisco. He'd gone back to living on the streets.

I often think about him and wonder how his life would have turned out if he'd remained in the church. I especially think of him whenever I drive through a fast-food restaurant. I want to ask, "Lassie, would you mind tradin' some vittles for some fine jewelry?"

But I don't have any piercings, my pirate voice is lousy, and I just don't have Danny's spirit.

Chapter Forty-Eight

The Blessing

Me and Maree - 1982

"**M**aree. Come see this!" I shouted from our living room. It was November 2016.

"What is it?"

"Hillary Clinton's giving her concession speech from the Grand Ballroom of the New Yorker."

"Really? How do you know?"

"The reporter said."

As we watched Hillary's speech the camera panned up to the crowded balcony.

"Wow, that's where we agreed to Father's match. I'm sure glad I said yes, back then."

"I'm glad I said yes too," Maree responded, after waiting a little longer than I would have liked her to.

Barely visible from behind the temporary screen set up onstage were the tops of molded plaster phoenix birds. The image brought back memories of June 1982.

"Michiko said there's a matching in Manhattan soon and you can go if you feel ready," said Danny, as we drove along a quiet North Dakota highway late at night. Michiko was the office secretary at our regional headquarters in Omaha.

"Really? That's a surprise. I'll have to think and pray about it. How soon does she need to know?"

"By tomorrow afternoon. A vanload of members is leaving Chicago the day after tomorrow."

Ready? How could I ever be ready to have someone, even Father Moon, suggest who I should marry? But it was clear to me that the western concept of romantic marriage was overrated. Several of my friends from Marysville were already divorced.

Danny pulled over at a roadside rest stop and I found a picnic table to sleep on. In the star-filled night, fireflies flickered nearby flying to and fro as crickets chirped, and a lone frog croaked in the distance. Anxious about the possibility of going to New York, I couldn't sleep. Closing my eyes, I breathed deeply, then said a short meditative prayer asking God what I should do. Seconds after opening my eyes a falling star shot across the sky. I took it as a sign.

"Wake up! No sleepin' on picnic tables allowed. What am I, your alarm clock?" yelled a tall, lanky highway patrolman, as the sun rose over a field of young corn. "Hey, weren't you on a table near Minot last week? Catch you again and you'll be sleepin' in the county jail."

After I woke Danny, who was sleeping in the Pinto station wagon, we were soon back on the road.

"So, we headin' to Omaha? What about that matching?"

"I'm goin'."

"All right!" Danny's face lit up in a big grin. "We can blitz our way there. Oh, by the way, soon after the matching there's going to be a marriage blessing at Madison Square Garden."

"Wait. Isn't there supposed to be a long waiting period after the matching until you get married?"

"I wouldn't know, I'm just a newbie! Hopefully you can get your questions answered when we get to Omaha."

As we worked toward our destination, I thought about some of the older members that were already matched. Craig's fiancée was a German missionary working in Jamaica. He kept a photo of her taped to the van's dashboard and would often read fondly from letters she sent. There were also others. They must be super excited about the Blessing. I was excited too. Married in a mass wedding at Madison Square Garden? Who gets to do that?

In Omaha, our regional director announced that the wedding ceremony would be on July 1st, but newly arranged couples would return to their missions and then join their spouses after a separation period. He explained that this was to honor the sacrifice of Korean wives who separated from their families for three years in the 1970s to do educational outreach. They had done so at the urging of Rev Moon and his wife who saw that Korea, and the world in general, was at a critical point where communism was poised to take over. To counter this, they had developed a successful initiative called Victory Over Communism (VOC).

I took a Greyhound bus with another matching candidate to Chicago, where we joined a vanload of members driving through the night toward the New Yorker Hotel.

We arrived in Manhattan just as the sun was rising and hours later, after hastily freshening up and grabbing something to eat from the van, we found ourselves sitting together in the Grand Ballroom of the New Yorker Hotel along with several hundred other members, listening to Reverend Moon speak, through a translator, on the importance of marriage, family and living for the sake of others. He urged us not to be superficial and declared that marrying across cultures and races would ultimately lead to world peace. It was the first time I had ever heard him speak and I was in awe.

As he continued, I pondered if I might get matched to one of the Japanese sisters. They were known for being kind, faithful, and determined. Also, my dad, who befriended Japanese prisoners aboard the USS New Mexico, would probably be happy to have a Japanese daughter-in-law.

We took a late afternoon break for lunch and returned to the Ballroom at 3:00 pm for the matching.

Seated on the carpeted floor, we watched as Reverend Moon asked for representatives from various countries to rise. He looked intently at each member and would then pair together some of those standing. But sometimes he'd glance out to those still sitting and match them to a person standing. When he came to an attractive New Zealand sister, he studied those standing and shook his head. Then he carefully scanned the room and pointed at me.

Me? I was in shock.

Rising from the sea of brothers, I joined the Kiwi to go to the balcony and discuss Father's match. My face was hot, and my mouth was suddenly dry as we sat down together, face to face for the first time. I felt nervous and overwhelmed.

"Do you love God and True Parents?" I blurted out. (Church members affectionately refer to Reverend and Mrs. Moon as the True Parents, since they are like a restored Adam and Eve.) It was all I could think of to say. Apparently, my old shyness around girls had returned, in spite of my supposedly improved social skills from all of the interactions on MFT.

When she said yes, I got up to leave.

Unfortunately, I hadn't given her a chance to ask me anything. Maybe I was afraid she'd turn me down.

Thankfully, she quickly said, "It's okay with me," as she got up to follow me downstairs to register our names and bow to Father and Mother Moon to signify our approval.

We were the third couple to accept our match. As we exited the ballroom we were greeted by a crowd of cheering brothers and sisters. For a few moments we joined the crowd as other freshly matched couples entered the lobby.

In a lull between cheers, I turned to my bride-to-be and said, "By the way, my name is Bob. And you are?"

"Maree, with two e's."

"Nice to meet you Maree, with two e's. Would you like to join me across the street at McDonalds for a cup of coffee?"

"I'd love to."

Maree was dark-haired and of medium build. She walked a little awkwardly but seemed like a good sister in spite of not being Japanese. And on the plus side, we wouldn't need a translator. Most of her Kiwi English was perfectly understandable. She also had pocket money which prompted me to introduce her to people as my financier as well as my fiancée.

In the days before our BIG wedding, we hung out together at the New Yorker, attended a Holy Wine ceremony, ate breakfast at a New York diner and visited churches in the Bronx. It was the first time either one of us had been on a subway. It was also the first time Maree had ever visited a Black church. She was impressed with their enthusiasm, sincerity, and love.

We also joined a huge rehearsal to prepare for the massive wedding. It felt like we were in a classic Cecil B de Mille movie.

Less than a week after meeting Maree, we joined 2,074 other couples in a record-breaking mass wedding ceremony in Madison Square Garden. It was exhilarating and I was delighted.

As we stood together near the front behind Mike (aka Peter) and his fiancée, I realized it was four years since I had joined the church. What if? I thought. What if I had hopped in the van that was leaving the weekend workshop near Seattle? But I didn't leave and here I was, getting married to a pretty lady from New Zealand.

Behind me in the packed auditorium were thousands of couples dressed in their wedding gear ready to pledge their unions to God and world peace.

Sure beats fishing in Alaska and living on a sailboat.

That evening, I wrote in my diary: ...I feel so unworthy to receive such a beautiful sister...I feel we will be able to work together very well...At first, I was kind of disappointed I wasn't matched to a Japanese sister but I have faith in Father.

Thirty-nine years. Four awesome children.

On July 1st, 2021, our thirty-ninth wedding anniversary, Maree posted a photo of the two of us on Facebook. It was a blurry picture taken on her phone in 2019 when we were in New Zealand promoting her memoir, Free Maree. She added the following:

Oh, we ain't got a barrel of money...but that's us, still side by side after 39 years! Happy anniversary Robert Gauper.

It's been amazing!!

Love you lots XxxxxX

Good photo or not, that post received over two hundred reactions and nearly one hundred positive comments. Next year we plan to be on a Caribbean cruise celebrating our fortieth with hundreds of our wedding alumni. Incidentally, the divorce rate of those taking part in that ground-breaking nuptial ceremony is less than ten percent.

It took a lot of faith to trust that Reverend Moon would choose a suitable life partner for me. But it wasn't just faith, it was the character of the candidates. Most of the church sisters I knew and worked with were women of obvious integrity, which was expressed in their purity and dedication to a higher purpose than themselves.

Father chose well. I'm always impressed by Maree's love for God, our children, and all people. She truly is a saint in my eyes. I know I couldn't have done better in choosing my own life partner, which is one of the main reasons why I've been so enraged with the bigots, and their supporters, who tried to take her away from me.

Chapter Forty-Nine
Snuff Ring and Darker Things

Ted Patrick - "The Father of deprogramming"

In January 1983 I visited my parents in Linda. My mother's two-pack-per-day smoking habit had caught up with her, and she was dying of lung cancer. I wanted to spend time with her before she passed.

Although mostly bedridden and a bit thinner than usual, her face was bright and cheerful.

On a rented video player, we watched *Jaws, The Sound of Music, Mary Poppins, Chitty Chitty Bang Bang,* and other movies in my parents' living room as a warm fire crackled in the wood stove.

"Watching movies at home, that's amazing," said Mom, in a raspy voice. "I'm glad that wasn't done when I worked at the *Bigfork Bijou*. We'd have gone out of business."

"Yeah, a lot of movie theaters aren't doing well. Remember when all of us went to see *Oh God?* I'm glad we did that."

"Me too. That was a nice movie. My Christian friend from AA won't watch it though. She heard it was unbiblical.

By the way, how's Maree? Her mother keeps sending me letters. She sure hates Reverend Moon and your church. I'm not a big fan, but you seem happy and fulfilled. At least you come home and show me movies. Mary, Maree's mom, says she never visits."

I sighed briefly. "Well, she'd like to, but she's afraid of getting kidnapped."

"I understand. Mary also sends me contact information for deprogrammers. It wouldn't surprise me if Maree's parents tried something like that."

I recoiled at the thought of anyone getting kidnapped, especially my wife. As my mother began to fall asleep in her recliner, I remembered back to the Seattle area workshop where I had first heard about kidnapping and deprogramming.

"Do you know where Mike is?" asked a tall, lanky blond guy dressed like a cowboy.

He looked like some of the students at Marysville High School who often wore blue corduroy jackets sporting *Future Farmers of America* logos.

"Mike? I don't know of any Mikes here."

"Someone downstairs said he brought you to the workshop."

"Nope. Peter invited me. Peter Saunders. Not Mike."

"Hmm...that's interesting. I'm all confused," the stranger muttered as he turned around to leave the room.

I noticed the name "CLINT" etched into his belt. Surprisingly, his back pocket lacked the telltale impression of a *Skoal* chewing tobacco snuff ring.

Later I asked Peter about my visit from Cowboy Clint.

"Who's Mike and who's that Clint fellow?"

"Clint's a church member from Montana and he's here to give some presentations. Mike is me. Peter's my alias."

"Alias? Why do you need an alias?"

"So I don't get kidnapped by my parents."

"Why would they do that? I don't understand."

"They hate that I'm in this church. They think it's a cult and that I'm brainwashed. I've already been kidnapped three times.

"The first time, it took four big guys, including my brother, to hold me down in the back of a van. I pretended I was deprogrammed after a few days, then ran away.

"The second time, I was kidnapped in Cedar Falls, Iowa and the third time was recently in Bremerton, Washington. Hopefully, they've given up by now, but I'm still worried they might try to snatch me again."

Aliases, deprogrammings, kidnappings. It was a lot to take in. How many of the others had aliases and were afraid of getting kidnapped? What would my alias be if required? Fred something? I'd also have to dye my hair. A redhead would be too easy to spot.

But it was crazy thinking. My parents would never have me kidnapped. For one thing, they didn't have the money. But more importantly, they trusted my decisions.

While my mother slept peacefully, I put a couple of small almond logs into the wood burning stove. The fire crackled and the pleasant scent of smoke filled the room. I could hear my dad's power saw whining outside. He had gathered wood scraps from the local dump and was transforming them into survey stakes.

Pouring myself a cup of coffee, I thought about another time, not too long after joining MFT in '78, when I had learned more about the twin evils of kidnapping and deprogramming.

Public Library.

The sign caught my attention as I walked down the street after getting kicked out of a Kmart parking lot in one of the smaller cities of Iowa, maybe Fort Dodge or Cedar Rapids.

Overwhelmed by all the accusations that I belonged to a cult and was brainwashed, I started to question.

Could I be brainwashed? Christians, Communists, rich, poor, young and old, everyone seems to hate us. Could all those people be right?

Lumbering zombie-like into the library, I directed my possibly brainwashed self to investigate.

In the *Cult Book* section, there was a generous array of reading material such as *Crazy for God, Kingdom of the Cults, Snapping,* and others.

To enlighten me in my current existential crisis, I picked *Let Our Children Go!* by fundamentalist-Christian-turned-deprogrammer Ted Patrick, *Crazy for God* by Christopher Edwards who had "escaped" from the Unification Church, and *What do you say to a Moonie,* a small booklet by Chris Elkins which I researched first, partly because it was the shortest.

Elkins had been a Unification Church member for two and a half years and had left on his own volition. As a Christian his primary argument against the church was theological. He also believed if the Moonies had received proper love and guidance in their own Christian churches, they wouldn't have joined a cult.

He was adamantly against kidnapping and deprogramming:

Deprogramming presupposes that brainwashing has taken place...I don't think that brainwashing is the method of the Unification Church. And deprogramming a person who has not been brainwashed can be dangerous...

Next, I studied *Let Our Children Go!*

Patrick, who is often credited as the "father of deprogramming," wrote in detail about his use of violence against so-called cultists, for example his kidnapping of a member of the New Testament Missionary Fellowship:

I reached down between Wes's legs, grabbed him by the crotch and squeezed hard. He let out a howl, and doubled up, grabbing for his groin with both hands. Then I hit, shoving him headfirst into the back of the car and piling in on top of him.

He once forcibly cut the hair of a Hare Krishna devotee:

"Just shut your mouth...Where's those scissors?"

Four of his relatives held him down and I cut off the tuft of hair they all wear on the back of their heads and I removed the beads from around his neck.

This reminded me of the history of anti-immigration thugs during California's gold rush, who would attack Chinese men and cut off their ponytails.

Patrick continued:

Then I picked Ed [the Hare Krishna] up by his robes and marched him backwards across the wall, slamming him bodily against the wall..." You so much as wiggle your toes again I'm gonna put my fist down your throat!"

Throughout the book, Patrick bragged about tying his victims up, spraying them with Mace, and limiting their sleep and food intake.

His justification for this harsh treatment? He claimed the cults practiced psychological kidnapping. He also preached against all forms of meditation and believed all "cults" are the same.

When I read his belief that cult members practice on-the-spot hypnosis I laughed out loud, earning disapproving looks from the library staff and patrons.

I suspected this book was a mixture of truths, half-truths, and wild fantasy. Furthermore, having had no education beyond the eighth grade Patrick lacked credibility, at least for me, as an expert on religious movements.

Crazy for God wasn't any better. It was loaded with melodrama. When I read,

Gotta get out. Got to...I'll do it at dawn. I have to escape, to escape for my life...

I felt like my head was going to explode from stifled laughter.

What about all those people who left after my first weekend workshop? They just got in vehicles and went back to the city. Guess that so-called on-the-spot-hypnosis wasn't working.

Inspired with righteous indignation, I exited the library with a new determination to fight the good fight and stand up for what I believed in. I wasn't brainwashed. If anyone was, it was those writers who churned out such trashy lowlife journalism. Either that, or they were promoting their

own agendas to justify their lack of faith as well as their bigotry and ignorance.

As I walked down the street in search of new fundraising area, the thought of me, a Moonie, getting encouragement from anti-Unification Church literature was amusing and even energizing.

Wonder what Ted Patrick would think of that?

❧

After visiting with my parents, I returned to a small fundraising team in the Midwest and continued to occasionally visit libraries in search of inspiration. Unfortunately, there was an abundant supply of negativity, not only in books, but in magazines and newspaper articles.

Of course, negative portrayals of my church weren't limited to print media. One day while meeting up with another team in a motel room we had the opportunity to watch the movie *Ticket to Heaven*, which happened to be playing on one of the TV channels.

"This is stupid and depressing. It's just a propaganda piece," said John from the visiting team during the opening scene. "Sure, some of it's true but it's taken out of context. I worked with the legal team in New York and follow this stuff."

"This stuff inspires me because it gets me so angry," I interjected. "Can you save your thoughts for afterward?"

John agreed and we huddled around the television screen to watch *Ticket to Heaven*.

It was like *Crazy for God*. Struggling with life, young man is tricked into attending retreat, gets brainwashed into following leaders and selling stuff to support cult. Two characters are conscience-stricken over enjoying a hamburger and milkshake. Loving parents snatch wayward offspring from dangerous cult to have him deprogrammed. After a few days, young man "snaps" back to worldly reality, renounces cult membership and rejoins beleaguered family to presumably live happily ever after.

"I could talk all night about what's wrong with this movie," offered John during the closing credits.

"Mostly it's a bunch of hyperbole, loosely based on a Canadian's experience with our church in Oakland. I happen to know the Canadian government helped finance the production. What right do *they* have to attack a new religious movement?

"Also, that deprogrammer character is obviously Joe Alexander Junior, whose father learned the faith-breaking trade from Ted Patrick. They're all in heaps of legal trouble and are now out of business. We don't have to worry about those goons anymore."

As John continued talking about the movie, I went outside to the van, which was where the brothers slept. It was a relief to hear about the convictions of Patrick and the Alexanders and I quickly fell asleep.

Tragically, those convictions led to the Alexanders searching for new customers overseas, where the rolling hills and green paddocks of New Zealand soon became their freedom-stomping grounds. The faith-breaking industry was about to impact me in a far more personal way. As my heart wrestled with thoughts of my mother dying, news came that would shock my soul to its core.

Chapter Fifty
Free Maree!

My wife's memoir

"Bob, your wife's been kidnapped," our Regional Director told me after our team arrived at our fundraising headquarters in Palatine, Illinois in August of 1983.

I'll never forget those shocking words.

It was a tough month. My mother was on her deathbed in Marysville, California, and I didn't know where my wife was.

Maree was kidnapped about a year after we first met in the Ballroom of the New Yorker Hotel. After our whirlwind courtship on the gritty summer streets of New York City and subsequent history-making wedding ceremony, I returned to the muggy Midwest while she flew back to Australia and eventually the winter rains of Auckland, New Zealand.

We communicated through letters and occasional phone calls, and I often sent gifts. She was especially impressed with the gold-plated Citizen watch and the custom-made beaded *Divine Principle* book cover, all acquired through my stellar bartering skills.

We slowly developed a fondness for each other and looked forward to starting a family together.

The announcement of her kidnapping was devastating, and I was livid.

Those jerks! Who the hell do they think they are? Stealing my wife!

"Why me, God!? Why Maree!?" I shouted out into a windless night outside an Illinois strip club I had been kicked out of, as a neon sign beckoned, "GIRLS...GIRLS!"

It isn't fair! I'm trying to do Your will, God. Why's this happening?

The sign continued flashing, rhythmically illuminating the dark parking lot.

Based on testimonies by my spiritual father and other church members who had escaped their captors, as well as my own independent research, I was extremely worried about Maree.

GIRLS...GIRLS...GIRLS!

Although anti-cult groups like CAN (Cult Awareness Network) portrayed deprogrammers as a benevolent bunch whose main concern was rescuing brainwashed people from dangerous cults, I knew better. "Protracted spiritual gang rape," Reverend Dean Kelly had called it, in an article about deprogramming for the *Civil Liberties Review*.

GIRLS...GIRLS...GIRLS!

At the least, I imagined she'd be imprisoned and tormented by disenchanted former members and anti-religious mercenaries after a quick buck. But she could also be starved, beaten, or even raped.

GIRLS...GIRLS...GIRLS!

If I'd really wanted to, I could have gone back inside as a customer (if I could get past the bouncer that just kicked me out) and spent my previously fundraised money on booze and gyrating women. Heck, maybe I could have traded a lap dance for a necklace and some earrings...

But I'd seen those kinds of guys in Tahoe and Vegas, and I knew I didn't want to be like that.

Thankfully, the fundraising van drove up and I could see the gleaming faces of my dedicated brothers and sisters, as the neon sign emblazoned them through the van's windshield.

Michael, our team leader, opened the passenger side front door to let me in. As I climbed inside the van, he said, "How ya doin,' Bob? You look a little down! I can't imagine being you. Your wife kidnapped and your mother dying. It must be really tough."

"Yep, it is," I agreed, settling into my seat, "but I'm not that worried about my mom. She's been in so much pain and it's time to let her go.

"But in Maree's case, I'm worried about what they might do to her."

Michael nodded gravely, keeping his eyes on the road. He knew what I was talking about.

"At first, I was angry at everyone and God, but I know it's not His fault. He must be angry too. I'm constantly praying for Maree," I continued. Summertime insects attacked the van's headlights as it sped down the dark highway. "I believe she'll get through this. She seems like a real trooper with tons of faith and conviction. She won't let those thugs break her down."

Soon I was proven right. Over a week after her abduction, I received a message to call the New Zealand church center.

To my surprise, a familiar voice answered when I called. It was Maree. "Bob, I've been rescued!"

The good news took my breath away.

"That's wonderful! So very, very wonderful!"

Tears of joy and relief blurred my vision as she continued speaking in that cute, quirky accent that I'd been afraid I might never hear again.

"The members stopped everything to focus on my rescue. I can hardly believe what they did to find me. The police were useless until they were forced to help.

"Also, I'm a celebrity. Everywhere I go people recognize me. My picture's been on TV and in the newspapers. Sarah, our church leader, wants to fly you out here."

"Really? When?"

"As soon as you can get your passport."

"Wow. That's exciting. I can't wait to see you!"

"Likewise. I can hardly wait either. Let Sarah know when you get your passport. She has a special mission for us, to visit my family together and try to smooth things over."

I gulped.

"There's so much to talk about," she continued, "but probably best to wait 'til you get here. Bye for now!" Long distance phone calls were expensive, so we had to keep it brief. "Bye."

It was a tremendous relief to know Maree was safe, and exciting to think that I would be seeing her soon. Hours later, my joy was tempered by another phone call.

"Bob, there's a call for you. It's your dad," said Scott.

Apprehensively, I picked up the receiver. "Hi Dad. What's up?"

His voice was somber. "Your mother passed away yesterday. I shoulda called sooner, but so much goin' on..." his voice trailed off.

The thought of my mother gone shocked me. My breathing slowed as I held back tears. I would miss her quirky sense of humor and biting wit.

"Thank you for calling now and for taking such good care of Mom. I'm sure it wasn't easy."

"No, it wasn't," he sighed through the phone. "She was never very healthy. There was always Something' wrong with her. Hopefully she's in a better place now."

I longed to pray with my dad and comfort him in his sorrow, but I worried he might get upset. He wasn't a praying man. Additionally, I wanted to share my joy of Maree's newfound freedom, but it didn't feel like the right time.

We talked some more, then said goodbye.

It was hard losing my mother at such a young age. She was only fifty-seven and all four of us kids were still in our twenties. She didn't get to meet her new daughter-in-law; I imagine they'd have gotten along well. I also knew that my potential future children lost a grandmother.

Mixed emotions of joy and sadness filled my days as the end of August grew near. I was looking forward to flying to New Zealand to be with Maree. Thankfully it didn't take long to get my passport and I was soon traveling to what the native Māori call *Aotearoa*, the "Land of the Long White Cloud."

Chapter Fifty-One

Land of the Long White Cloud

New Zealand travel poster 1910 - 1959
N. N., Public domain, via Wikimedia
Commons {{PD-US-expired}}

The muffled droning of jet engines lulled me to sleep as I lay across the seats of the half-full plane flying to New Zealand, having switched carriers in Hawaii after a ten-hour flight from Chicago. In around nine more hours I'd be arriving. Although worried that I'd be too anxious to sleep, thankfully that was not the case. When the captain announced we'd be landing in Auckland soon, I was well rested and ready for the adventures ahead. A flight attendant armed with tongs was passing out steamy heated towels. "Good morning," she said cheerily.

WELCOME TO NEW ZEALAND. A large sign greeted passengers as we walked down a corridor toward the terminal. Two middle-aged women were serving free cups of hot tea to weary travelers, and I gladly accepted.

This is flavorful. Sure beats Lipton tea bags. What a nice gesture.

After I claimed my luggage and went through customs, a handsome young Polynesian brother greeted me.

"Hello, Bob. My name is Seti. Welcome to New Zealand."

"Hi. Thanks for picking me up. How'd you know who I was?"

"I only saw two passengers with red hair. The other one was a woman."

We walked toward his car.

"I'll put your baggage in the boot."

Baggage? Boot?

He opened the car trunk and I put away my luggage then headed for what I believed to be the passenger door.

"Um, I'm driving, mate. You'll have to get in the other side. Steering wheel's on the right here in New Zealand."

As we drove away from the airport, Seti said, "Maree's teaching at our farm. I'll take you there after we check in at Headquarters. How about I shout you some breakfast on the way?"

"Uh, shout?"

"It means I'll buy."

"Thanks. That'd be nice."

As thoughts of what type of native culinary treat, I might soon experience made my mouth water, we approached a circular intersection and Seti drove directly into it without stopping. I recoiled slightly, worried that cars might hit us. Three quarters around the circle, we exited.

"What kind of intersection was that? I'm only used to stop signs and lights."

"That's a roundabout. You don't have those in the States?"

"Never saw one. Seems to work well, although I'm glad *I'm* not driving."

After stopping in a parking garage that Seti called a car park, we were soon strolling around downtown Auckland. It was a pleasant, cool day and the blue sky was dotted with numerous clouds. The people walking the streets were a mixture of Caucasians, Polynesians, Asians, and an occasional Black person.

My stomach began to growl as I continued to anticipate where we might stop to eat. An inflight magazine had filled my mind with images of interesting shellfish, meat pies, and fish and chips. But it was breakfast time. Maybe we'd stop at a pub for a mixed grill which could be lamb chops, sausage, egg, bacon, and chips. And if the pub was health conscious it might include a grilled tomato and onions.

"You first," said Seti as he opened the door to a ...McDonalds.

McDonalds? I'm on the other side of the world and the first place I go to eat is a McDonalds? It just didn't seem right, but I didn't complain, at least out loud. As we stepped up to the counter, I ordered an Egg McMuffin and a coffee.

"White?" the counter person asked.

Thinking she might have said "What?" I responded, "A coffee."

"White?"

Confused, I glanced at Seti.

"She wants to know if you'd like cream in it."

"Yes, please. White."

As we sat eating our American meal Seti told me that he was Samoan and had been in the church a few years. His mother was also a member. He explained that Samoans have a tradition of following the advice of their adult children.

"That's different. Too bad that isn't a tradition in Maree's family. Obviously, *you* didn't have to worry about getting kidnapped."

"No, I didn't," said Seti, between sips of coffee. "Maree was always worried that would happen to her, and it did. It's hard for me to relate. But she pulled through. She's excited about your visit."

"I'm excited to be here. Although I'm rather terrified about meeting my in-laws." My stomach squirmed at the thought.

Finished with our meals, we returned to the car, and again I tried to enter on the driver's side.

"Hope I don't keep doing that."

"Don't worry. Happens to all the Americans."

A few minutes after leaving the "carpark," we were driving past the University of Auckland.

"Chris and I go there. I run a martial arts class."

He looked rather fit and trim, and I figured it must be from doing martial arts.

"And we've been trying to set up a student ministry," he continued. "Lots of people are against it, especially the Christians and communists. Strange bedfellows if you ask me," he chuckled.

Soon we were entering a tree-filled park.

"This is the *Auckland Domain*. I'm taking the scenic route."

"It's beautiful and so green. What type of tree is that?" I asked, pointing to one with a twisting, turning trunk and exposed roots that looked more like a large vine than a tree.

"I think it's some type of fig. There's a huge one growing further inside the park. And that's the Auckland Memorial Museum, on our right."

Minutes after exiting the domain, we parked in front of an elegant two-story Victorian building.

Grabbing my *baggage* from the *boot*, we went inside and were greeted warmly by Sarah, the national church leader.

"Welcome to New Zealand, Mr. Gauper. Nice to see you again." We had met briefly at the time of our Blessing the previous year. "You'll find it a lot less hectic here than in New York. Especially since there's not a mass wedding taking place. Seti, please put his baggage in the brother's room, and thank you for picking him up."

"And shouting for breakfast," I added, proud of myself for using the native lingo.

"Let's go into the sitting room for a brief chat," said Sarah. "Did you have a nice flight?"

"It was great. Slept a lot of the way."

"Good! I heard about your mother's recent passing. My sincerest condolences."

"Thank you."

"Seti probably already mentioned that Maree's teaching at the farm. It's a nice place for her to be right now. I'm hoping both of you can help heal the rift between her and her parents. Also, as you are probably aware, there's a chance they could try to abduct her again. So, you'll also be her protector."

"I'll do my best."

"But we'll talk more once she's back. Meanwhile, let me introduce you to Frank and Margaret."

A red-haired brother was lying on the floor, fixing a clothes dryer.

"G'day. Welcome to New Zealand," said Frank as he sat up and shook my hand. "Nice to see you. I'd get up, but I've got a crook leg. Know anything about dryers?"

"Not really. Didn't have such a luxury growing up."

"Me neither. They're fairly simple though."

As we chatted about electric versus gas dryers, a door opened nearby and out walked a young lady. She had dark hair, thick eyeglasses, and delicate features.

"Hello," she said in a soft, gentle voice. "You must be Bob. I heard you talking. I'm Margaret. Maree and I are good friends."

"Would you please show Bob around upstairs?" said Sarah.

"Glad to."

Margaret led me up to the kitchen, dining room, prayer room, and the brothers' room where my *baggage* was. The building was spacious but modestly furnished.

"This used to be the queen of Tonga's New Zealand residence. Hundreds of neighbors signed petitions to try and prevent us from moving in."

"Wow. Like the opposite of a *Welcome Wagon.*"

"What's that?"

"Uh, it's a service that greets new residents with a gift basket from local businesses."

"The *un*welcome wagon. That's what greeted us."

We walked out onto an upstairs balcony. The street below was quiet, but I could hear traffic close by. Most of the nearby dwellings appeared to be small, upscale apartment complexes.

"So, how did you meet the church?" I asked.

"Through my mother. My sister Jenny joined in England and Mum was impressed with how it benefited her. Mum's also a member, you might meet her at Sunday Service."

"Wow. You and Seti are such a contrast to Maree's situation."

Margaret chuckled briefly. "Well, supportive parents are somewhat unusual here too. We have our fair share of hostile ones.

"So, that's the upstairs tour. You'll be heading to the farm with Seti after lunch. Perhaps you'd like a little rest in the brothers' room? Someone will knock you up when it's time to eat."

Knock me up? I refrained from telling her what that meant in America.

Inside the room, curtains swayed gently from an ocean breeze. I lay down on a small bed and pulled a thin wool blanket over me, reflecting with amusement all the new words, expressions, and unexpected experiences.

It was especially thrilling to know that I'd soon see Maree again. It had been more than a year since we'd parted in New York. I took a picture of her out of my wallet. She looked radiant with her bright eyes and dimpled smile. I was so proud of her and felt I had hit the jackpot in the matchmaking gamble.

As I gazed at the photo, my longing for Maree was gradually overshadowed by dread at the thought of meeting her parents. The cool air entering the room was especially welcome as I began to sweat. My heart rate increased, and my mouth became as dry as a summer sidewalk on the Las Vegas strip.

Suddenly I felt like a condemned prisoner heading for the gallows.

Chapter Fifty-Two

Knocked Up

Closing my eyes, I tried taking deep breaths to calm my uneasy spirit. Images of meeting Maree for the first time flashed into my mind's eye, along with scenes of hanging out together in and around the New Yorker Hotel. Manhattan memories, from a happier time.

Knock...knock.

Must be knock up time?

I put Maree's photo away, then joined the others in the dining room.

After someone offered grace, I bit into a toasted cheese sandwich and encountered an unexpectedly strong, salty taste. Peeking between the bread slices I saw what looked like dark brown axle grease.

"An acquired taste," smiled Seti when he saw me inspecting my sandwich. "It's called Vegemite."

The taste didn't take long to acquire. I took another bite and liked it.

Wow. I've only been here a few hours and there's so much to share with Maree. I can hardly wait.

"Okay pardner. Time to hitch up the wagon and mosey on outta here," said Seti as he got up to leave the table, mimicking a line he must have heard in a Hollywood Western.

I grabbed my things and walked to the wagon... station wagon. This time I remembered to get in on the proper side.

We moseyed our way down residential streets, past quaint houses with mostly tin roofs, through some roundabouts, then turned onto a street marked *Motorway.* Somewhere along the road a large highway exit sign that read *Manurewa* grabbed my attention.

"I know we're on our way to a farm, but why would they name some place after animal dung?" I wondered out loud.

"Huh?"

"Manure-wa?"

Seti laughed. "It's pronounced muh·noo·ree·wuh.

It's a Māori word. Something about a drifting kite. Nothing to do with manure!"

After about an hour on the two-lane freeway, Seti turned onto a narrow, paved road, and we were soon driving alongside a wide, meandering river similar to the Sacramento River in California.

We continued down the winding road past rolling green hills and small farms, then along a short dirt road.

"This is it," said Seti as he drove up to a small white house and stopped. A black and white cow watched as we exited the wagon and went inside the farmhouse.

It was empty.

"I noticed the van was gone. They're most likely all out at the beach, although Maree's still here, anticipating your arrival and preparing for her next lecture. I phoned her before leaving Parnell. She's probably in the prayer room studying," said Seti.

He walked up to a door and tapped on it. A female voice I recognized answered, "Come in."

Seti motioned for me to enter the room.

Instead of studying, it appeared that Maree had been on the floor praying. She looked up, nervously.

Finally! I get to see my beloved! Her dimpled smile and bright spirit melted my heart. Cliché or not, absence had indeed made my heart grow fonder.

She began to stand up, but before she could, I sat next to her on the floor and sang a little song I had written for her. It was about keeping ourselves away from "the other side," the side of despair, faithlessness, and doubt.

My singing helped both of us overcome our initial nervousness and we were soon chatting away.

"How has your first day in New Zealand been?"

"Interesting. I've learned about roundabouts, tasted Vegemite for the first time, had 'white' coffee at a McDonalds and learned about *manure-wa*. I've even been knocked up."

Maree smiled and blushed slightly.

"I'll be right back," she said, moving toward the door.

Returning with a small book, she handed it to me and I chuckled when I read the title,.

"This'll come in handy. I read through it and know what 'knocked up' means in America," said Maree.

"Thank you. I'll study it right away. Seti said you're giving a lecture soon."

"Yes I am, in about fifteen minutes."

"Well then, I'd better let you be."

After taking a short stroll around the farm I entered the lecture room. Several people were already there, and I introduced myself. Before long, Maree walked in and began her lecture titled, *The Mission of the Messiah*. Her knowledge, confidence and presentation skills impressed me.

And to think those jerks tried to destroy her faith! How dare they! I silently fumed at the thought.

"Good job," I told Maree after we sat down together.

"Thank you. By the way, did you know we're going to be guests on Radio Pacific...it's a popular talk show."

"Really? If I'd known *that* I might have stayed in America. You know I'm the strong, silent type."

"So you say. But I heard you speak in front of that church in the Bronx. You'll do fine."

Beneath my façade of shyness, I was actually rather excited at the prospect of being on a radio talk show. I was about to learn that the purpose of my coming to New Zealand was not just to attempt to build bridges of peace with Maree's family but also to be part of a major Public Relations exercise.

Chapter Fifty-Three
Guess Who's Coming to Invercargill

Keith Richards - 1995 - Public Domain Image Wikimedia Commons

Back in Auckland, our session on *Radio Pacific* went well. The host was cordial and staunchly defended us against callers who were in full-on attack mode. We were on several other radio stations and interviewed live by various reporters. A nationwide newspaper, the *New Zealand Herald,* quoted me (in reference to our large group wedding) on their front page:

"At least I have lots of people to remind me of my wedding anniversary."

"Look at this," said Sarah, placing a newspaper in front of me as I took a bite of Vegemite toast and sipped a cup of tea in the dining room. It was an article about Maree and me, which included a photo of us in the lobby of the New Yorker. The caption referred to me as her "church husband."

"Church husband? Who's ever been called that?"

Sarah smiled reassuringly. "Probably no one. But technically they're right. You're still not legally married. Lots of members took care of that right after the Blessing. Too bad you and Maree didn't."

"We talked about it, but there were hundreds of church members visiting city halls in Manhattan and nearby. We also heard we needed a blood test. It would have taken more time than we had."

"Well, we'd better fix that right away. I think a trip to the Registrar's Office is in order to get you properly married. Especially so you can be next of kin in case they try to kidnap her again."

Oh wow. I hadn't even thought about that. Feeling confident I could ward off any would-be abductors, I would be the knight in shining armor for my fair princess.

"Sounds good. When should we do that?"

"How about in a couple of hours? By the way, you both have been doing great dealing with the media. It's possibly the best publicity we've ever had."

Our legal marriage at the Registrar's office was a joyous, light-hearted occasion. When the Registrar asked if I'd like to kiss the bride, I quipped, "No thanks. I'll wait." I really wanted to, but we were still in our separation period. Only hand holding was advised.

The busy days helped keep my mind distracted until I was finally sitting next to Maree on our flight to meet the Ryans (now officially my parents-in-law) in her hometown of Invercargill, an encounter I had been dreading, and for good reason. My right leg shook uncontrollably. Noticing my nervousness Maree squeezed my sweaty hand and shouted, "Don't worry, you'll do fine!"

"You don't have to yell," I reminded her gently as I pulled away her earpiece.

Invercargill is New Zealand's southernmost city, a flat, provincial place of around 50,000 mostly Caucasian inhabitants. Guitarist Keith Richards reportedly called it the "arse-hole of the world" after a concert at the Civic Theater in 1965 during which Invercargillites showed more interest in singer/songwriter Roy Orbison than in the Rolling Stones.

The closest city, Dunedin, is almost a three-hour drive away, although Father Pat, Maree's uncle, could make it in two. Richards called Dunedin a "black hole" and a "tombstone" after visiting one rainy Sunday. "I don't think you could find anything more depressing anywhere," he wrote in a memoir. And *that* was summertime.

My stomach churned like the nearby ocean and gray clouds swirled past our window as we descended. The plane landed then taxied toward the small terminal building where several people had gathered to meet passengers.

It was a windy day, and I was surprised to see men wearing shorts, with what appeared to be woolen sweaters. When the plane stopped, workers wheeled a metal staircase next to the plane and passengers began to disembark. As we saw Maree's parents waiting for us, she squeezed my hand again for comfort.

With obvious discomfort and mixed emotions, the Ryans greeted their estranged daughter and shook the sweaty hand of her "church husband."

As for me, it was a moment of supremely squirmy self-consciousness and serious awkwardness. This was probably how Sidney Poitier's character would have felt when meeting his white future in-laws for the first time in the 1960s film *Guess Who's Coming to Dinner*.

As we began the short drive to Maree's family home, I stared out the window so I wouldn't have to look at the couple sitting in the front. *These are the people that tried to break up my marriage. Do they have any idea how much I adore their daughter? How am I supposed to forgive them?*

While absorbing the new urban landscape I couldn't help noticing the power poles were made of concrete rather than wood.

As we pulled into the driveway off Leith St., Maree said, "Dad built this house. He built others in Invercargill, too. Maybe he can give us a tour sometime."

The home was impressive: five bedrooms and a large upstairs recreation room with pool and ping pong tables. Unfortunately, by the time Mr. Ryan had completed all the upgrades, his children had already started leaving the nest.

While touring the custom-built dwelling I passed a small bookshelf filled with anti-cult literature. It felt like I was back in the US revisiting the cult section of a public library. The familiar scurrilous titles were all there: *Snapping, Let Our Children Go, Kingdom of the Cults, The Moon is not The Son.* I had read them all, but it still made me nauseous.

Way to make a guy feel welcome.

Was this how a Jewish man might feel, showing up at his in-laws and seeing *Mein Kampf,* or a Black man stumbling upon a KKK handbook? I had to wonder.

Other manifestations of passive aggression became apparent as we endured visits from Maree's relatives, of whom there was such a multitude it was hard to keep track. One night, one of the many uncles came over for dinner with his wife. The mood was tense.

"Got your seed potatoes in yet, Paul?" asked the thin uncle, as we sat together around the large dining table where, in a past era, seven Ryan children must have gathered for meals.

"Already in the ground," replied Maree's Dad. "Gotta have 'em ready for Christmas."

"And how's your golf game, Mary?" asked the aunt, who was rather heavy-set.

"Not bad," said Maree's mother. "Now that the weather's lovely I'll be getting out more."

No one asked about *my* hobbies. They probably thought Moonies had no time for such frivolity, which was partly true. But they could have at least wondered, *So Bob, what did you like to do before you got brainwashed?* But no. They didn't even enquire which state I was from, or if I had family back there. Consequently, no one learned that my mother had just died, less than a month ago. It was as if we weren't even there.

Thankfully, a trip to a sheep farm was different.

Maree's aunt cooked us a feast and was warm, friendly, and encouraging, as was her family. The kindness and the rolling green hills and fresh country air were a welcome respite from chilly, overcast Invercargill.

Old friends and neighbors were also friendly and supportive. "You got a good man!" boomed a tall Irishman who had lived on the same street as the Ryans for several decades. Meanwhile, our efforts to heal the rift between Maree and her parents weren't going well.

One day, as I showed off my best pool shots to Maree in the recreation room, I could hear footsteps coming up the staircase. It was Mrs. Ryan.

"Like to play some table tennis?"

"Sure," I replied, thinking she was being friendly.

Instead of a casual game of ping-pong it felt like she was there to do battle. Maree's slightly built, gray-haired, fifty-eight-year-old mother attacked the small plastic ball with precision, gusto, and repressed anger. After humiliating me for three matches, she laid down her paddle and said, "Enough of that. I'd better check on the potatoes," then walked away.

Maree and I took a short walk around the quiet neighborhood. Although the air smelled of burning coal, it was nice to be outside as the brisk wind blew and the evening sky darkened.

Returning to the Ryan home we saw Maree's dad tinkering in his workshop. He was building a small ornate cabinet.

"Your work is really impressive," I commented, observing several pieces of furniture he had made.

"It's a hobby of mine. I like taking old, discarded pieces of native wood, and turning them into useful objects. I'm especially proud of this jewelry box." He reached up and grabbed the box and handed it to me.

It was a miniature chest of drawers. It was beautiful and I was amazed at the detail and craftsmanship.

"I'd love to get back into woodworking myself someday. I took woodshop years ago and really liked it."

Mr. Ryan sighed. "How would you do that? Don't you people need approval from Moon for everything? Just live a normal life. Why do you have to follow that man anyway? All you have to do is live by the Ten Commandments."

I wanted to ask, "If that's the case, why do you need the Pope? Or Jesus?" but didn't want to get into an argument. We politely excused ourselves.

After a few more torturous days we were heading to the airport to go back to Auckland. Maree's dad was driving, and she sat in the front beside him. I gazed out the side window as I had on the day we arrived. Those concrete power poles reminded me of a saying:

Some people's minds are like concrete, all mixed up and permanently set.

That seemed like an apt description of my in-laws; and that being the case, it was so hard for me to love them. But for Maree's sake, I would do my best.

It helped if I tried to put myself in their shoes and ask myself what I would do if I were them, or what I would be like had I lived my entire life down there, in the arsehole of the world?

Chapter Fifty-Four
Barter Bob

It felt like our visit had been mostly a waste of time. There had been no Kumbaya moment where barriers melted away. Nothing had essentially changed in their feelings toward us and our church.

Maybe it would be different once we had children — their grandchildren. But that would not happen until much later.

"What's wrong?" Maree asked, this time without shouting since she didn't have her headphones on, as our plane headed toward Auckland.

"Now that meeting your parents is over, I have a different kind of dread. Soon I'll be back in the US, selling stuff. I've been on MFT for over five years. It used to be exciting, and I really felt God's presence. Now it's just a chore and I really want to do something else."

Maree squeezed my hand, nodded, and said, "I'll pray for you." She leaned back in her seat and closed her eyes. I did likewise and we both fell asleep.

Returning to MFT, after visiting New Zealand and spending time with Maree, was even more difficult than I expected.

I was on a team of mostly sisters peddling oil paintings in large cities and this country boy hated it. Lester's team was supposed to be made up of "artists" traveling around the country selling our art, and the art of others. When I joined his team, he handed me a stack of silk-screened canvases.

"Pick the artist you want to be."

Looking through the pile I didn't see any stick figures that *I* could have drawn.

"Sorry, I don't see anyone I could be."

Annoyed, Lester grabbed the pile, picked a silkscreen signed *J. R. Scott*, and tossed it to me. "Be this guy."

I became J. R. Scott. Wasn't even sure if J.R. was a guy. Could've been a Janice, or a June. Most likely the artist was a Chen, Li or Han since the art came from Taiwan. I wasn't comfortable pretending to be an artist and did terribly on the team. My record was three days without making a single sale.

I missed Danny and our escapades as a two-man team throughout the Midwest and felt useless. Until one day...

"What's going on? I'm calling the police!" a man with a strong East Indian accent yelled from the doorway of our motel room in Southern California.

"Please don't do that! Let me explain," I countered from behind the blankets that were hanging from the middle of the room, as I started putting on my trousers. My words were wasted. He was already heading for the office.

"Everyone up! We're in big trouble," I yelled as I ran barefoot out the door.

He was picking up the phone as I burst into the office.

"We're missionaries raising funds for our church. Please don't call the police."

"Missionaries shouldn't be defrauding innkeepers. There's only supposed to be one person in that room! You need to be taught a lesson!"

He started dialing.

"Wait. We've got some nice pictures. I could give you one."

"Pictures? Pictures of what?"

"Mostly oil paintings."

"Hmm. Okay, I'll look at what you have." He hung up the phone. "They'd better be nice. I still might call the police."

I went to the room, put on my shoes, and grabbed a carrying case full of oil paintings.

"When Lester gets back, tell him I'm in the office keeping us out of jail."

"What's going on?" asked Bonnie.

"I'm giving the motel owner a painting, so he won't call the police."

Ignoring her shocked expression I rushed back to the office, sat the carrying case on the counter and opened it.

"Flip through these and pick one. You can have any one you want."

As the motel owner flipped through the paintings, my mind wandered to the previous day when we had had a memorable incident involving firecrackers.

"Get out with your hands up!" a police officer shouted from his megaphone as three others aimed their shotguns at us.

They had parked their patrol cars at the bottom of the hill and hiked toward our van.

The six of us inside the van obliged and got out.

"Now turn around. Lean against the van and spread your legs!

What's in your hands?"

"Sandwiches."

"Sandwiches?"

"We're having lunch," responded Lester.

"What's goin' on here? A jogger reported hearing gunshots."

"That's my fault, officer," I said. "I was lighting firecrackers."

"Firecrackers? Where'd you get them?"

"Traded for 'em in South Dakota. But I don't have any more."

The officer came closer, looked down at the spent firecrackers and shook his head.

"Put your hands down. Go ahead and eat your sandwiches. Besides eating lunch, what are you doing?"

"We're artists traveling around the country selling paintings," said Bonnie with a smile. "Let me get you something to drink. You must be thirsty after your climb up the hill." She grabbed some cold apple juice from the ice chest. "Would you and the other officers like to look at our paintings?"

I can't believe it. She's going to try and sell these guys something.

As the officers drank their juice, Bonnie, our team's top seller, placed paintings on the grass.

"John, I've seen your apartment. It could really use some decoration," said one of the officers.

"These three are a set. They'd probably look great in your apartment," said Bonnie, pointing.

He looked them over and bought the set.

A short while later, all four officers had bought paintings which they then rolled up for their walk down the hill. It was more than I had sold in a week. As they started to leave, the officer with the megaphone looked over to me.

"Stop playing with firecrackers. They're dangerous and illegal."

"I'll take this one. It reminds me of where I grew up in India."

Sheesh, that was close. No telling what the police would've done if they encountered us again!

As the motel owner rolled up his painting, I saw Lester drive past the office and park by our room.

"Is that your boss? Tell him to never come back here again. Unless he pays full price of course."

"I doubt we'll be back. We're based out of Chicago. Now the weather's warming, we'll be working our way back there. But if we do come back, let's talk about trading for rooms. I've bartered for motel rooms many times. I'm always trading for something. That's why I'm called Barter Bob."

"If you do happen to be back in the area, let's talk about it. Have a safe trip back to Chicago. And don't rip off any more motel owners."

"That's not my call. But I'll tell the boss what you said."

When I returned to the room, Lester was scowling.

"What the heck happened?"

"I was getting dressed when the owner barged in yelling. He threatened to call the police. I bribed him with a free painting so he wouldn't."

"Let's get outta here," Lester cut me off irritably. "That fella might change his mind."

Everyone quickly grabbed their stuff and took down the blankets hung up to separate the sisters' sleeping area from the brothers'. We were soon in the van. As we drove away the motel owner stared at us and smiled when I waved.

I patiently waited for a thank you from Lester. Like: "Wow, Bob! Quick thinking, trading that guy for a room."

But it didn't happen. I shouldn't have expected any encouragement. We weren't exactly fond of each other.

Ever since I joined his fundraising team about a month earlier, he made fun of me for listening to bluegrass. Hillbilly music, he called it. It didn't help that I was the worst seller on his team. He even persecuted me for reading my New Testament which I always carried in my shirt pocket.

Lester drove us back up the hill where we had the firecracker incident, to have breakfast and restock our selling cases for another day of hawking. I only had to replace the painting I'd given away to the motel owner since I hadn't sold anything the previous day. *Why bother?* I wondered silently, flipping through the inventory. Finding a replica of the painting I had given away I grabbed it and realized it also reminded me of where I grew up: the sun rising behind a mountain range, a tractor plowing a field while farmworkers labored nearby, waterfowl flying in the distance. I was mildly homesick but knew I wouldn't be happy back in Linda. I'd be so bored. I dreaded the idea of another day trying to peddle artwork in Southern California. *What should I do?* Seconds later, my question was answered. "We need to talk," Lester said as he tapped me on the shoulder then walked toward the front of the van as I followed. "This is for you. It's a train ticket back to Chicago. You've been picked to work in the fish business."

Chapter Fifty-Five

Shooting Stars

Andromedid Meteors - France - 1872 Amedee Guillemin

"You'll be in Chicago a short time then on to St. Louis to help open a new seafood store," said Lester.

I let out a sigh of relief as I took the ticket. We got into the van and began eating our breakfast.

Lester announced the news to our team. Everyone was happy for me because they knew how much I struggled. In a short while, Lester dropped me off at the train station and wished me luck.

"You too," I responded. We didn't have much else to say.

As the train meandered its way through the Los Angeles metropolis, I remembered being a bearded long-haired liberal hippie with a backpack holding all my belongings, which included a small stack of New Age spiritual books, on the train from Portland to Seattle.

Now, all my possessions were inside a Samsonite suitcase, and I was so clean-shaven and clean-cut I'd sometimes been mistaken for a Mormon missionary.

I pulled the New Testament from my front shirt pocket and flipped through it, stopping to read quotes I had underlined. A passage in Ephesians stood out:

You were taught, with regard to your former way of life to put off your old self...

I'd certainly done that.

No longer was I the shy, cynical person in search of a more adventurous and meaningful life. Now I was a confident, outgoing young man with a dream, a purpose, and a wedding ring on his finger.

I remembered back to when I stood on a picnic table in a crowded outdoor market shouting, "I am a Moonie!" and another time when I was standing on a wooden box, street-preaching in downtown Manhattan while an old man pelted me with his cane.

It had been over five years since I had excitedly knocked on my first door in Seattle, fundraising for my church.

So many memories. So many tribulations, as well as victories: freezing in sub-zero temperatures, struggling through chest-high snow drifts; the arrests, beatings, and persecution; the hatred and kindness of strangers; the joys and challenges of working closely with brothers and sisters.

I had met thousands of America's people, from homeless Native Americans singing *God Bless America* inside a Minnesota jail cell, to well-off businessmen parading down Rush Street in Chicago with their trophy wives.

I'd been inside a small humble cottage at the end of a dirt road in Wisconsin and sold fake flowers at Chicago's Sears Tower which at that time was the tallest building in the world.

As night fell, I looked out my window while the train chugged through the desert. Nearly everyone was asleep in the darkened car. A star shot across the sky.

I had seen so many falling stars while lying on top of my old van in Nevada, or on rest stop picnic tables on MFT.

It was outside my old travel trailer in Linda while lying on a cot and staring up at the Milky Way that I first asked God what I should do with my life. I saw a shooting star and took it as a sign.

The train stopped in Ogden, Utah and several families came aboard. A young couple with two children sat in seats across from me. I smiled and nodded at the father. He nodded back and probably thought I was a Mormon.

Some day that will be me, with my wife and children.

I was excited about joining the seafood business. Ever since I decided to leave my hometown of Linda to head toward Alaska to work on a fishing boat, I believed an ocean related future was my destiny, although I was surprised that destiny would begin in St. Louis, hundreds of miles from any ocean.

I was especially inspired that my hopes and dreams concerning the ocean aligned with Reverend Moon's.

Fish Business. What's that going to be like?

Chapter Fifty-Six
St Louis Fish House

Fish Business - 1984

I had just locked the glass door from the inside and was about to head for the upstairs apartment where some of us slept.

Knock, knock... Knock, knock.

Although it was after 9pm and pitch dark outside, I could see the shapes of people partially illuminated by the light from inside the St. Louis Fish House in the suburb of Ferguson, a short distance from the famous downtown arches.

I unlocked the door and opened it. Standing in front of me were six middle-aged African Americans.

"Sorry we're late. We drove all the way from Alton, Illinois. Heard you had the best fried catfish in St. Louis. Could you please serve us?"

It had been a busy Friday night and I desperately wanted to go upstairs to rest. But how could I turn them down following that?

After letting my new customers in I relit the fryer, split six small, skinned catfish in half, dipped them in my secret recipe batter, then coated the battered pieces with spiced cornmeal and breadcrumbs. The hot oil bubbled and crackled loudly as I dropped in the wild-caught catfish that was faithfully brought to us twice a week from rural Tennessee, iced down inside wax-coated cardboard boxes in the back of an old pickup truck driven by a thirty something mountain man with scraggly dirty blond hair and missing teeth. (I tried using farm-raised cat, which was cheaper and more size and quality consistent, but Black folk didn't like it. "It don't have no taste.")

Before long, six happy customers left the store carrying individual Styrofoam containers filled with French fries, coleslaw, a piece of bread, a container of hot sauce, and two pieces of the best fried catfish in St. Louis.

In addition to African Americans, the store attracted a significant Asian clientele since my business partners were Japanese, and they knew their fish. Often, Midwesterners would enter the store just to stare at the array of seafood most locals had never seen: whole flounder, bright red loins of sashimi grade tuna, live geoduck clams from Washington State squirming in the fish case and Maine lobster swimming around in the area's largest live lobster tank. I was proud of this store which I had helped build.

One day I got a phone call.

"I'm calling to complain about your shrimp."

"Really? We've never had complaints before. What's wrong with it?"

"I served it at a cocktail party, and no one would eat it. I found uneaten shrimp in ashtrays and the garbage."

"How long did you cook it?"

Long silence.

"Oh...I thought it was already cooked."

After that, I decided to organize and teach some seafood cooking classes. They were appreciated and well attended.

One day, when I walked into a nearby hardware store that I frequented, an employee motioned for me to follow him to the back.

"We ben wondrin', why you hirin' Niggers?" he whispered. "Can't you find white guys to drive your trucks?"

Disgusted and speechless, I shook my head, quickly found what I needed and left.

Three decades later, African American Michael Brown would be shot and killed by a Ferguson police officer and the "Hands up! Don't shoot!" protest movement began not far from where our fish store was located.

Thirty years later, at one of those protests outside the front of Sacramento's Memorial Auditorium, a young black man gave me a bear hug.

Chapter Fifty-Seven
Country Roads

In 1986, it was time to end my career as a fish-frying monk. I left the St Louis Fish House to join Maree in New Zealand and we began our life together as a couple. (Normally wives moved to their husbands' locations but Maree, being an assistant to a National Leader, was deemed to have higher priority.) It was exciting to live in such a beautiful country on the other side of the world and it was wonderful to finally experience the joys of being a married man.

On December 11, 1987, I became the proud and nervous father of a beautiful red-haired girl.

We lived nearly four years in New Zealand together, doing various kinds of church work. For a while I was selling metal etchings and large framed photographs throughout the North Island out of my small Daihatsu minivan; I also worked as the assistant manager of a seafood department at a grocery store. I fathered another beautiful baby daughter.

But I was restless and frustrated with the lack of career opportunities. Also, the Korean church leader in charge of New Zealand kept assigning me to fundraising teams even after I explained that I'd done five years of MFT and was burned out with it. I started having frequent migraine headaches.

Eventually I made the hard decision to leave New Zealand and return to the St. Louis Fish House. After her U.S. visa came through, Maree and our two young daughters joined me there for two years.

Just as it must have been for many Japanese wives, it was a huge culture shock for Maree, coming from her small island country to a large American city. She had to learn how to drive on the opposite side of the road, adjust to a new climate and a new regional dialect, among other things, all while facing the normal challenges of raising two small children far away from any familial support networks. Through her own strong character and sheer determination, she adapted and survived, without a lot of help from me, as I mostly focused on work.

Being a father was great. It was nice to enter our small apartment after work, to shouts of "Daddy's home!" The girls were so cute and bubbly. The older daughter reciting *Georgie Porgie* with her strong New Zealand accent was especially charming.

Sometime in the early 1990s we learned that many church members were returning to their hometowns at the encouragement of Reverend Moon. It was daunting to consider another move, yet California tugged at my consciousness. For a while I prayed about it and struggled to know whether that was the right direction for us to take.

One day, listening to a sermon on audiocassette tape while delivering seafood in Nashville, I was struck by the words of Dr Mose Durst, a beloved church elder: "We need to get out of our areas of comfort and challenge ourselves." During the same trip a song played on my truck radio that seemed like an answer to prayer. It was a country song by Lionel Cartwright about taking a leap of faith and casting away your doubts. The first step would be the hardest. My future was suddenly clear.

We boxed up most of our belongings and stored them, with arrangements for friends to ship them later.

I bought and modified a large trailer into a smaller trailer that I would tow behind our Dodge Colt station wagon. The custom-made trailer carried two large plastic collapsible insulated fish boxes for our essentials. We traveled light as we said goodbye to St Louis.

✺

Boonville. The highway sign along Interstate 80, about two hours west of St. Louis, got my attention because the church had a farm and workshop site in Boonville California where many Unificationists joined.

"I thought Boonville was in California," said Maree.

"It is. Looks like it's in Missouri too. Let's exit the freeway here and you can get to see some of smalltown America."

After quickly driving through Boonville, we were on a two-laned highway driving west toward Kansas City, enjoying the scenery.

When I started singing John Denver's *Country Roads* song, Maree protested.

"Please stop. I hate that song! One of my kidnappers sang it on our way to the deprogramming."

"Sorry, I didn't know." She rarely ever spoke of that difficult time. I switched to *You Are My Sunshine,* hoping that wouldn't trigger any painful memories.

Behind a beat-up pickup that was traveling about forty miles an hour, I complained, "Come on Grandpa. You can drive faster than that."

"Is that my grandpa?" our four-year-old asked from the backseat.

"No dear. Your daddy just calls old men that. We're not in California yet."

I smiled at Maree then carefully passed the truck. Our daughter waved at the driver and "Grandpa" waved back.

After a couple of days of "Are we there yet?" questions from the back seat and reminders to "Yock your doors" whenever we stopped, our beige-colored, trailer-towing Dodge Colt passed a *Welcome to California* sign.

"Almost there! We'll be at Grandpa's in less than two hours."

"Is he our real Grandpa?" our oldest asked.

"Yes honey. He's your real Grandpa," I replied.

Our fully loaded vehicle, with the 1500 CC Mitsubishi-made engine, lumbered up I-80 past Truckee.

"I lived here as a toddler. And Grandpa helped build this freeway we're on," I informed my family.

While climbing Donner Summit I educated everyone about the mishaps of the Donner Party.

Finally, we made it to the mountain's crest.

"It's mostly downhill from here," I exclaimed as we sped toward my hometown. Little did I know just how downhill things were about to get.

Abruptly, I heard something behind me and investigated through the rearview mirror. *A wheel was wobbling and suddenly flew off the trailer.* Sparks flew as the trailer's axle ground into the pavement. I watched in horror as a lone wheel sped past me down Grandpa's I-80.

Chapter Fifty-Eight
Downhill

Wide-eyed, I watched my insubordinate trailer wheel continue downhill as I pulled over to the shoulder of the road. Thankfully, before it was out of sight, I saw it shift to the right, roll off the freeway, then up a dirt embankment and into the forest.

After I turned on the emergency flashers and set the parking brake, I took deep breaths, closed my eyes, and briefly rested my head on the steering wheel.

"We'd be much safer out of the car," I said as vehicles sped by.

We gathered in the weeds a safe distance away.

It was like a scene out of the *Grapes of Wrath*. Our stricken vehicle sitting motionless next to the freeway while my stunned wife sat on the rough ground, our two-year-old on her lap and our four-year-old resting her head on Maree's shoulder.

"I'd better go find that wheel," I told them, trying to sound cheerful.

Jogging down the hill, I soon found skid marks where the errant wheel had left the pavement. Following the trail up the steep embankment I found it lying next to a small pine tree.

I carefully rolled the nearly 30-inch diameter wheel through the trees toward I-80, but at the top of the embankment I slipped on wet leaves and lost my grip on the tire. It sped down the small hill and back onto the freeway!

"Dammit!" I cried out while brakes squealed as motorists avoided the hazard. I watched in horror as the tire started rolling further down the busy Interstate. It occasionally scraped against the concrete barrier separating east-bound traffic from west-bound and continued speeding downward. Soon it was out of sight.

Extremely worried it might cause an accident, I ran downhill. After about ten minutes, I could see my wheel rolling towards me near the highway barrier. Thankfully, a small rise in the road had changed the direction of the wayward object.

At the valley where decline met incline I watched as the tire traveled uphill, then downhill, then back again.

Up...down...up...down...up...down, a hypnotic pendulum. Up, down. Up, down. Up, down, taunting me like a mischievous child. Finally, it stopped, leaning against the median barrier. When the road was clear of traffic, I dashed over to grab it then hurried back to the shoulder.

God, please help me get this thing and myself safely back to my family. Please watch over them.

With my arm tightly gripping the over forty-pound wheel, I trudged uphill toward my car and family. It took about twenty minutes of climbing until I could finally see them. Surprisingly a car was parked in front of the Colt and people were standing nearby. Someone started running toward me.

"Here. Let me carry that for you," the young man said as he grabbed the heavy weight from my aching arm.

There were three other young men near the car. Four good Samaritans had stopped to lend us a hand.

"How can we help?" one of them asked.

"You can help me get this wheel back onto the trailer. In my rush to leave St. Louis it looks like I failed to check the lug nuts. Luckily, I have spares."

In less than ten minutes the wheel was snugly back on the trailer. After making sure the other trailer wheel was securely tightened, I motioned to my wife and kids.

"Come here please. Let's thank these nice young men." After I shook their hands, I saw Maree bend down and whisper to our girls. They shyly said, "Thank you for helping us."

Our saviors smiled brightly, nodded their heads, and watched as we got back inside our little station wagon. As I drove away, I looked into the rear-view-mirror.

"Were they angels, Daddy?" our oldest asked.

"Maybe so."

Dad was sitting at a table inside his fruit stand at the corner of Highway 65 and State Street in Wheatland, cracking walnuts, when I pulled in front. It had been over two years since he'd seen our small family when I had come to California to pick up Maree and the children from their flight. He smiled, then stood up. He had gained a lot of weight since I last saw him and was wearing an eyepatch.

"I expected you quite some time ago. When you phoned from Reno, I thought you'd be here sooner."

"I thought so too. I'll tell you what happened later. In the meantime, say hello to Maree and your grandkids."

"Mind if I give 'em a Tootsie Roll Pop? I give 'em to customers' kids."

"That'd be fine. I'm sure they'd love one. I see you've put in a bathroom. Why'd you do that? Can't you just use the one in your trailer next door?"

I watched my dad's face darken to a scowl.

"The damn health department made me. Said I need facilities for employees and customers. Only employee I have now is Kay, on the weekends. For a while, they let me slide with a porta-potty, then shut me down a week before Memorial Day, busiest weekend of the year. I threw out boxes and boxes of spoiled fruit."

His face began to redden, and I felt sorry I'd asked about the bathroom, but he continued, eyes blazing.

"Victor from the trailer park helped me build it and install the sink and toilet. Health department inspected it and turned me down. Said I need *wheelchair* access.

"God was I pissed. Victor tore down the walls and redid it, so now I have a bathroom that's almost as big as the fruit stand. Assholes!"

In front of a rickety table topped with small plastic baskets of fresh tomatoes, plums, and peaches stood my two children and their mother. Dad walked over to them with a large plastic jar filled with Tootsie Roll Pops.

"Pick one."

The kids shyly picked blue ones. He then held the container of chocolate-filled hard candy on a stick in front of his daughter-in law.

"No thanks."

"Sorry 'bout the language. Now that you and your kids are here, I'll have to watch myself." Maree nodded in agreement then asked what happened to his eye.

"I have glaucoma. Supposed to have surgery someday."

"Sorry to hear that. Does it hurt?"

"Not if I keep the patch on."

"May we use the bathroom?"

"Of course. Don't get lost though."

After the bathroom break, Grandpa showed us around his twenty-year-old, one-bed-room, single-wide trailer which included a custom-installed piece of OSB chipboard that had replaced a window.

Suddenly I had a sinking feeling in my stomach that I was back in Linda. After all, it was only twelve miles down the road.

"You gonna start a business helping people with their window problems in Olive-hurst/Linda?" I quipped.

Dad chuckled. He had little pride when it came to his accommodations.

As I stared at the small living room with the grimy carpet and foldout hide-a-bed couch, I wondered how my wife and two kids could survive in the small space. Would my wife struggle here in Yuba County like my mom had? Would my children? I began to doubt the wisdom of returning home, but consoled myself with the thought, *at least this is only temporary. We'll be out of here soon and things will improve.*

I was wrong.

One thing we hadn't anticipated was that California was only just pulling out of a serious economic recession. We ended up spending seven months in those cramped, grubby quarters. It was the "worst of times." Several job opportunities fell through; one daughter ended up in a body cast after breaking a femur while falling from a swing; we were denied unemployment benefits. Then Maree began suffering from morning sickness.

"Bob, I'm pregnant."

To say I was overwhelmed seems like an understatement. Things were hard enough already without another responsibility. But I also felt bad for Maree.

My Dad liked to get up early and fix bacon or hamburger meat for breakfast in the same room where we slept. Maree would wake to the nauseating smell of greasy meat cooking, then try and keep from throwing up while taking care of our two little girls, who took turns at sleeping on the recliner or in the sofa bed with us. Mostly she remained stoic and uncomplaining. When we learned we were having a little boy, she began to feel better about the pregnancy.

Then, just when we felt like our situation couldn't get any more challenging, my brother got out of jail and needed a place to stay.

He slept in our Colt.

Somehow, we survived. We sold flowers in bars and nightclubs, and at corner stands on Valentine's Day, and did palm-readings (long story). While Maree started teaching piano at the local military base, I took whatever job I could, from wrenching cars in Oakland to plowing rice fields for a local farmer. Eventually when I had better jobs we moved into an apartment. It was only about 700 square feet, but after Dad's trailer, it felt like a palace.

Finally, with some assistance from my in-laws, we were able to buy a house where Maree, with my encouragement, opened a successful piano-teaching studio. The house, on Wheatland's Main Street, sat on a large lot which was a short walk from the fruit stand.

The property included a small "granny flat." Years later, my dad would join us there.

Maree took several short-term jobs as a church organist or pianist. Eventually she got a regular gig at Grace Episcopal, a short walk from our house. Grace became our adopted church home. We also visited other churches from time to time and got to know many of the local pastors. This was something Rev Moon had encouraged his followers to do.

We had two more beautiful children, both boys. The last one was blessed with flaming red hair just like his proud dad, but fortunately minus the Charlie Brown size head to go with it. Eventually all four moved away to college.

Chapter Fifty-Nine

Hugged by God

Sacramento Protest

California being so far from the Midwest, my time as a fish-fryer in St Louis soon became no more than a distant memory. Until one day in 2014, a shocking news report jolted my attention right back to Ferguson, MO. A young Black man named Michael Brown had been killed by a policeman and the whole town was an uproar. Sadly, it didn't come as a complete surprise to me as I'd been painfully aware of the simmering racial tensions in that part of the country. I wished there was something I could do; however, I had another project to focus on: religious freedom and the American public's apparent passive acceptance of deprogramming and its practitioners. Ever since they attempted to break my wife's faith back in the 1980s, I had been on a self-imposed mission to blow the whistle on these guys. Unknown to me, my crusade for justice would bring me into close contact with the events unfolding back in Ferguson, MO.

It was 4:00 in the morning and I couldn't sleep as I anxiously thought about what I should wear.

Is it going to rain? Should I bring an umbrella? If I bring an umbrella, how am I going to hold it and a placard, and hand out fliers at the same time? Maybe I should just stay home.

But I knew that the last wasn't an option; my conscience would bother me too much if I didn't go. Even if I only got a picture of myself holding up my *TED Enables Defamers* sign in front of the Crocker Art Museum in Sacramento, it would be worth it. Besides, some people had already heard I was planning to be there to protest a TED event at twelve noon on December 12, 2014, so I needed to show up.

A recent Ted Talk featured a woman who admitted to being a deprogrammer. That alone irked me, that TED would even allow such a speaker. But even more upsetting was that the same woman, in her talk, claimed that Unification Church members had their brains altered by a "memetic viral infection" and proceeded to compare us with Hitler Youth and the followers of Jim Jones (who died from poisoned Kool-Aid in a mass suicide).

I was incensed. No number of comments or emails could get that talk removed from public platforms and it already had over a million views. I had to do something.

Since I couldn't sleep, I got up and worked on some signs and fliers. After my son woke up, I talked him into going to Sacramento with his sixty-year-old rabble-rouser dad, so that he could be my driver, photographer, and bodyguard. We loaded up the car and, although the sun was out, I grabbed a rain jacket. Soon we were cruising past walnut orchards and the welcome sight of overflowing creeks and ditches, hopefully a sign that California's long drought might be coming to an end.

As we drove between some rice fields I watched in awe as copious flocks of waterfowl flew near us and landed nearby. I then rolled the car window down a short way and listened to the music of ducks, geese, swans and other birds as I closed my eyes and took some deep breaths of the rain-washed air to calm my nervous spirit.

Before long, my son was practicing his big-city driving in downtown Sacramento. After some difficulty, he soon had the car parked. I grabbed my four signs, to give to any others who might join me in my protest, and we walked a couple of blocks to the museum entrance. I held my *TED Enables Defamers* sign under the words *Crocker Art Museum* as my son took a photograph.

I had already checked out the museum on Google Street View and had toyed with the idea of standing near the entrance and giving a speech condemning TED's support of forced thought reform, also known by the euphemism, "deprogramming"; but since there wasn't a captive audience waiting in line at the door, I nixed my public speaking plan, held up my placard and started handing out fliers. The fliers read:

Who's in bed with TED? You might be surprised! Find out at Who's in bed with TED? | LeavingLinda.com

Thanks to a suggestion from my son, I had added a QR code that linked to my recent blog post which detailed some of the history of forced thought-reform and questioned why TED would support such sordid activities.

In a short while, as expected, museum security was telling me I couldn't be there and that I needed a permit to protest. I informed them that it was my constitutional right, and they would need to have me arrested if they wanted me to stop. I then threw my car keys to my son and told him to make sure he took lots of video if the cops came. The security guards, a lady and young Black man, then left me and went back inside.

Sadly, it appeared no one else would be joining me in my protest and it was going to be a one-man show, so I decided to put down my placard with the other ones I had made and focused on giving out my fliers. I simply welcomed people to TED and handed them a piece of paper. I guess everybody must have thought I was with TED because nearly everyone took one. People were even asking me what entrance they should go into, and I was happy to direct them.

However, before long, Mr. Head Security Guy was telling me to get off the museum property and forced me into the street, which wasn't all that bad, although I did have to loudly explain to passers-by that I was banned from the sidewalk and that if they wanted to know why, they should come over and get a flier from me. That seemed to work because most people took the extra effort to get a flier. (A few times I did disobey my orders and quickly jumped over to the sidewalk, handed out a few fliers then hopped back into the street.)

"The last time I was doing this at a TED event, my wife joined me," I told the young security guard standing near the door keeping an eye on me. "She's a piano teacher and has a recital tonight, so she was too busy. She was kidnapped and held against her will by hired faith-breakers years ago because her parents were upset that she left the Catholic Church, joined a different church, and married me. We do what we can to let people know that TED supports kidnapping and forced thought-reform."

"Where does she teach?" the guard asked.

"In a small town about fifty minutes north of here," I responded.

It started to rain softly, and I was glad I brought my rain jacket. More people walked by, and I continued to joyfully welcome them to TED and hand them a flier. At 1:00pm I had ten fliers left of the original stack of 139 (I had given one to a curious Staples clerk). I wished the friendly security guard a good day and walked away, jumped in the car and soon we were heading home.

I quickly checked my blog when we arrived home. Fifty visits to *In bed with TED?* between the time I left home and came back, which was about three hours. Not bad and I'd probably get even more visits later. Little did I know, another very special moment of validation was yet to come.

The next day, my wife and I attended a Christmas concert by the Sacramento Choral Society and Orchestra. I don't often go to such things, but I was attempting to acquire a little more culture, besides the "agri" kind. So, there I was, traveling to the big city again, this time with a car-pool of friends from Grace Episcopal Church.

The five of us, having left our vehicle in a downtown parking garage, were walking toward the auditorium, where the concert was to take place. As we drew closer, the muffled sound of a megaphone pierced the night air. When we rounded a corner we saw police cars, flashing red lights and a large group of people chanting loudly and holding placards that read "Black Lives Matter!" All of this was being closely watched by a small army of uniformed police officers. What we were witnessing turned out to be a protest and "Die In" against the recent shooting of unarmed teenager Michael Brown in Ferguson, Missouri. The protest was taking place right outside our concert venue.

The atmosphere was tense, as a long line of concertgoers snaked into a side entrance, while a much shorter line filed toward the front of the auditorium, right past the protesters. I encouraged our party to head over the lawn and to the short line in front. Soon, there we were, standing a few feet from the noisy crowd. Close by, a young African American man held his arms high while shouting, "Hands up! Don't shoot!" It was the security guard, now in street clothes, who had been keeping an eye on me while I was at the Crocker Art Museum! We recognized each other instantly.

"You the man!" he shouted happily. "You were out there protesting all by yourself. He was doing that for you, right?" he asked my wife and she nodded yes. "By the way, how was your piano recital?"

"It went well. Thank you for asking."

He then took a short step and gave me a bear hug. And there we were: a graying red-headed, brain-infected white guy and a young African American male, embracing as shouts for justice rang out from the crowd and echoed off the Memorial Auditorium walls. It felt like...I was being hugged by God.

And suddenly, the restlessness and anxiousness of the previous day washed away, like the fading quack of a lone mallard as it flies desperately to join the flock.

Chapter Sixty

Eye Patches in the Holding Tank

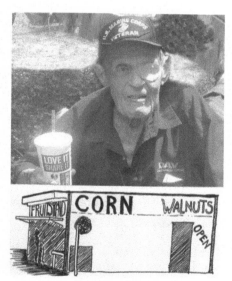

Dad and his fruit stand

"Hundred dollars? That's all you got? Where's the rest?" The young punk asked as he held a gun to my dad's head after pushing the eighty-year-old to the tattered carpet floor of his trailer.

"That's it. That's all I got. Fruit stand business ain't like it used to be."

"Think you're funny? I've a mind ta shoot you right now. You better not be lying!

"Finding anything?" the miscreant yelled to his partner who was ransacking the bedroom.

"Bunch o' junk and some Vicodin!"

"Take that and let's get the hell outta here!

"Semper Fi," acknowledged the criminal as he nodded toward my dad's *Retired Marine* cap. Dad watched as his attackers bolted out the door. For years afterward, he swore those guys would've killed him if they hadn't known he was a Marine.

I was helping at a church retreat in the San Bernardino Mountains when the attack happened and didn't hear about it until days later when I phoned my wife from a pay phone.

"Grandpa's been robbed. Some jerks knocked him down inside his trailer. He's in our cottage now. Yesterday a television crew came by and he told them what happened but refused to go on camera."

"Is he all right?"

"Still pretty shaken up and finding it hard to sleep. I said he could move inside but he's not interested. Keeps calling on the intercom asking when you'll be home."

"Okay, I'm flying out tomorrow. I'll be back in the afternoon."

"Good. He'll be happy to hear that."

As my flight headed toward Sacramento, I remembered a time when I had taken Dad into Marysville for some errands, which always included taking fruits and vegetables to Brandi at his bank and to the doctor and staff at the cancer clinic and other places around town.

On the way back home, I stopped at *Food for Less,* a large discount food market in Linda.

"What can I get you? Stuffs a lot cheaper here than at *Big Al's.*"

"Don't need nothin'. Just take me home."

"Okay. I won't be long."

When I got back to the car, he said, "Stop at *Big Al's.* I promised Jessica some tomatoes."

I should have known. No wonder he didn't want to go to Food For less.

Jessica, a young cashier, and other staff greeted my father as we walked through the small grocery store in Wheatland.

"Hi John!"

"Afternoon, John. Is that your son?"

"Here you go, John. Two barbecued chicken and a bag of ribs."

It was the butcher that handed him the chicken and ribs, each foil package marked with a black Sharpie, "$1.00."

"Save me a few ribs. You keep the rest," said Dad when I dropped him off at his fruit stand.

"Thank you. Why does that guy give you such a deal?"

"I bring him fresh produce and he saves me the barbecue that didn't sell the day before."

"*Big Al's* already has produce. Why does he need to get it from you?"

He stared at me as if I'd asked him the stupidest question in the world.

I should have known better. Grocery store produce couldn't compare.

In addition to bearer of good fruit (and vegetables) Dad was a rescuer.

He married my mom, a frail tuberculosis survivor, and took her to California, saving her from the harshness of Minnesota winters and her overprotective parents.

His humble trailer and fruit stand became a refuge for many: stranded motorists, Mexican farmworkers who sold cracked walnuts for Christmas money, the trailer-park prostitute who would sit and talk, and even a young Moonie family who were temporarily displaced.

He gave away free flowers to people on their way to the cemetery, special produce discounts for customers with large families, and small jobs for kids at the trailer park. Once a part-time employee stole a business check and tried to embezzle $500 from his checking account. The police caught the single mother, but Dad wouldn't press charges.

"She must've been desperate."

Stealing from Dad? That's like stealing from Santa Claus.

For his safety, and because his old trailer was falling apart, we'd been encouraging Grandpa to move onto our property. However, he wouldn't budge. It took the home-invasion robbery to finally move him. Once I was back home, I helped him settle into the small cabin which sat behind our house.

It was comforting to have him nearby and was especially good financially for our kids.

He had contracted the extremely rare filariasis disease from a mosquito bite while serving in the South Pacific, which left him with constant leg pain. After years of persistent paperwork, he received a military disability payment. That, along with Social Security and an Operating Engineer's pension, combined with low living expenses, left my dad with substantial discretionary income.

Our boys would fight over who'd run errands for their grandpa to *The Village Pharmacy* or *Big Al's* since he always gave such generous tips.

One day, I was the only one home and he needed some items from the grocery store. When I got to the store, I looked at the barely legible writing. Included on the list was *Horse Radish* and *Chicken Ice Cream*.

I found horseradish but the odd ice cream request had me stumped.

"Sorry, I couldn't find any chicken ice cream. What's that?"

"You know what it is. I'm always buyin' it," said Dad, gruffly.

"Sorry, Pa. I don't know."

"It's those chocolate covered ice creams with the pointy cones."

"You mean Drumsticks?"

"Yeah...of course! And you got the wrong horseradish."

"That's the only kind they have."

"No it's not. You shoulda asked the butcher. He keeps the kind I like in back."

"I'm supposed to know that? Here, hand me the horseradish, I'll return it, then talk to the butcher and get your Drumsticks."

Sheesh. Next time, I'm waiting for the kids.

"I need more room," Dad exclaimed one afternoon.

I couldn't argue. He was an enthusiastic fan of mail order companies and it showed. His tiny cabin was crammed full of stuff.

"I'd like to buy this trailer." He circled a classified ad in the *Appeal-Democrat* newspaper and handed it to me. It was a twenty-eight-foot travel trailer with slide-outs. In less than a week I had it parked in our back yard next to my garage.

To take care of the sewage, I buried a one-inch diameter PVC pipe that led to our household drainage system. Then I installed a macerator pump on the trailer's holding tank, the theory being that with the push of a button, the macerator would energize, then pulverize the waste and pump it through the buried pipe. And it worked, for about two minutes.

After removing the macerator for inspection, I could see it was clogged with eye patches, band-aids, paper towels and cigarette butts. I pleaded with Dad and his hired house-cleaner to please stop throwing garbage into the toilet. Those pleas were ignored so I designed a technique using wire mesh to prefilter the sewage.

Nothing says "I love you Dad" like screening through his sewage searching for eye patches, I thought when first testing the system.

"Hello! Anyone there?" Dad's voice kept calling from the intercom. It was close to 3:00 AM.

Barely awake, I answered, "Go ahead, Dad."

"Someone's bangin' on my door! Can you come out and check?"

"Yes, Dad. I'll be right there," I yawned.

The trailer's porchlight was on and no one was knocking on the door. I went inside.

"Ask her what she wants."

"Who?"

"The lady."

"What lady?"

"This one right here!" he said impatiently, gesturing toward an empty space next to the bed.

"Uh, what do you want?" I asked the invisible woman, but before she could answer I was startled by a sound behind me.

Knock, knock. The trailer door creaked open slowly as I looked for a weapon.

Thankfully, it was Maree.

"How's it going out here?"

"It's okay. Say hello to Dad's visitor."

Maree looked perplexed.

"There's a lady next to the bed," I explained.

"What does she look like?"

"Like *that,*" said Dad, agitated and pointing into thin air. "She's got a face like an alarm clock." Then he chuckled, "I never did see a lady with an alarm clock on her face before. And there's cats up on the ceiling."

Neither Maree nor I could see cats on the ceiling or the strange woman by the bed.

"Thanks for checking on us, Maree. I'll spend the rest of the night on Grandpa's couch and keep an eye on things."

"Sounds good. I'll go back inside and try to get some sleep. Good night, Grandpa."

As I tried to rest in Dad's living room for what was left of the night, I could hear him carrying on a conversation with himself or whoever. I didn't know if they were spirits, dementia, or too much Vicodin.

One day, he soiled himself but yelled at me angrily when I tried to help him. I didn't know what to do and called my sister, whose husband, Jim, had experience dealing with old people.

"Call the fire department and let them take care of it. There's nothing else you can do." I followed Jim's advice, not realizing this would be my dad's last day in our backyard.

Half a dozen or more EMTs and firefighters showed up from the local fire department. Dad was surprisingly friendly to them and enjoyed the attention as they wheeled him into an ambulance and drove him to the hospital for observation. A doctor recommended moving him to a convalescent home.

It was a hard decision. My wife and I sincerely believed in the three-generation family, but Dad needed professional care. Thankfully, there was a bed available in a care home close to my sisters' homes in Rocklin. They visited him nearly every day. On January 7, 2016, at the age of ninety-one he passed away.

Dad's gray metal casket descended slowly into the rain-soaked earth as two Marines in dress uniform began folding the American flag which they had draped earlier over the coffin lid. The sound of *Taps* rang out through the cemetery as another Marine played his bugle. Suddenly a fighter jet thundered and circled above us as I solemnly received the folded flag.

My tears flowed freely, like a broken water main.

The casket made a quiet thud when it stopped descending, and the Marine hushed his instrument. The plane roared away.

Then silence.

Chapter Sixty-One
Shooting Star Thistles

Memorial to Daniel Farris

"If you like meat, try the barbecue," a young man offered as he heard me, my son and my wife discussing what Korean food we'd order as we looked over the menu at the *Ocean Fish and Chips* restaurant in Marysville.

I smiled at my wife. We'd been eating Korean food since that customer was in diapers.

"Thanks for the tip," she responded.

We were on our way home from an afternoon outing to the Gray Lodge Wildlife Area near Gridley.

Our youngest son was on a winter break from UC Berkeley and had offered us an *All-inclusive dinner out, Korean or cuisine of your choice* as his Christmas gift. We chose Korean.

It had been a pleasant afternoon, although a bit cold for late December in Northern California. Thankfully I brought the gloves which Juan, volunteer director of the *Western Farm Workers Association* in Yuba City, had given me for a Christmas present.

Growing up, I never visited the refuge that was just a forty-minute drive from Linda. If I wanted to see waterfowl and wild animals, I only had to go to the dredger ponds. Now I try to visit Gray Lodge at least once a year.

From a sheltered observation building we had looked out onto a large pond filled with geese, ducks and a lone egret patiently stalking its prey nearby. A group of sparrows flitted back and forth from the pond's shoreline to a small tree. Beyond the pond sat the Sutter Buttes outlined by a gray and white painted sky, and I recalled my youthful escapades inside the long-abandoned missile silos.

For the journey back to Marysville I drove through Gridley towards Highway 70. Before crossing the Feather River, I pointed out the humble farm labor housing to the right.

"I helped distribute food there last summer."

"Those homes look pretty basic," responded our son, a socialist. "In the richest state in one of the richest nations in the world, our farm workers should be housed better."

I agreed.

Before his passing, Reverend Moon encouraged his followers to embrace head-wing thinking: to combine the best of both right-wing and left-wing ideals.

Most of my church life, I had been a card-carrying Republican and supported right wing causes. Before joining the Unification Church, I was more left leaning. To become a *head-winger,* I had to find a middle way, where I could understand and appreciate both sides.

With that in mind I began volunteering with the *Western Farm Workers Association* in Yuba City. The dedication and sacrifices of the volunteers were impressive. Their idealism reminded me of young UC members.

Meanwhile, at the Korean restaurant, I decided on bibimbap. Maree ordered spicy pork and our son, a vegan, picked fried oysters ("Oysters don't have faces," he explained), as well as an order of tteokbokki (spicy simmered rice cakes) to go.

We savored the meal, along with the rare and precious moments with our youngest child.

For Christmas we gathered informally for tacos at my sister Karen's beautiful place in nearby Roseville. Both of my sisters raised families successfully and are now enjoying their grandchildren. The happy sounds of young children filled the spacious home.

Our brother Greg did not have such a happy ending. Having spent most of his adult life as a transient who bounced continuously from jail to rehab, he died face-down in a ditch outside of Oroville in early 2016. He was 58.

On New Year's Day Maree, our son and I went on another trip: a five-mile hike to Beale Falls, after driving the thirty-minute trip from our house to the trailhead.

It was a beautiful, warm winter day after a week of rain and fog. We took our time hiking up to the waterfall past rugged oak trees and other flora, stopping to watch birds or take in the scenery.

I'd been to the falls many times as a teenager, but only in the summer, to go swimming, jump from the top of the falls, or sometimes gawk at hippy girls skinny-dipping in the cold water or sunning themselves on the rocks.

It was nice to be here in January and not have to worry about sunburn, rattlesnakes, or other distractions.

As we climbed higher near the riverbank, we could hear the gentle roar of the waterfalls and continued hiking upward. Finally at the top, I walked to an oak tree and held onto a metal cross placed there in remembrance of a Daniel Farris who had died after jumping from the falls in 2009. Gingerly I looked over the one-foot-high chain link fence, which was far too short to protect or deter anyone, into the pool about fifty feet below me.

Did I really jump from here? I couldn't remember the exact spot. It was over fifty years ago. Mickey and his brothers would have been with me. But I couldn't ask them, they were all dead.

My heart raced just thinking about it, although I was probably less scared doing that than the first time I walked into a bar selling flowers for the Unification Church.

Our son wandered down a rocky path with his binoculars and camera to explore the area. Maree was sitting on a rock resting. "Look, my step-counter is almost up to six thousand," she announced proudly.

Her once-dark hair was now more of an ash blond, and her face carried some tell-tale lines; but my wife was still a good-looking woman, and I was proud. I sat next to her and held her hand, grateful she had joined us on our hike.

Mist floated up from the turbulent pond below, coating the jagged rocks nearby. I could smell the humid air. A young couple walked by carrying small children on their backs and I remembered when Maree and I were that young. How time does fly, more like a jet plane than a bird. In a few months we would celebrate our fortieth wedding anniversary.

On our way back to the trailhead, we stopped beside an open field.

"Is that pussy willow?" Maree asked, pointing to a scraggly dried out plant with cotton-like tips.

"No, it's star thistle. An invasive weed that's everywhere. My dad said it came here in shipments of alfalfa seed from overseas, long ago. It's almost impossible to get rid of. Bees love it and star thistle honey is highly prized. Mickey and I used to have shooting contests with the flowers."

"How'd you do that?"

"We'd wrap the stem near the prickly blossom then yank on it, propelling the thistle through the air. I was amazed how far some of them flew."

I went on to describe how sometimes, after swimming in the Yuba River to wash itchy peach fuzz off us, Mickey and I would stand on the shoreline shooting star thistles into the water. "

"One of those might have floated to the Sacramento River, then on to the Pacific Ocean." I mused. "It could have gone all the way to New Zealand."

"That would be impossible."

"About as impossible as me meeting you."

Maree smiled a contemplative smile then held my hand as we continued toward the parking lot where we unpacked a picnic lunch inside my 1996 Ford Econoline van, which stood out among the fancy Priuses, Subarus, shiny late model pickup trucks and SUVs that probably cost nearly as much as my house.

Our oldest daughter who now lived in New Zealand had sent us a *Fix and Fogg* nut butter assortment for Christmas. I'd made sandwiches from the *Everything Butter*: hemp, almond, peanut, pepita, chia, sesame, sunflower and flaxseed, with sliced banana on homemade whole wheat buns, and cups of piping hot tea. It was a little taste of heaven on earth and soon we were driving back home.

The gravel road was rougher than usual from the recent rains, with water-filled potholes and washboard bumps. At one point a small stream flowed down the middle of the road and crossed to the other side. On our left we passed a cove from Camp Far West Lake where I often used to take our children and guests on my old pontoon boat. One time the boys and I stayed on it overnight. I remembered being amazed at how bright the moon was that night. It was nice to see the lake full again.

That evening, our son asked if I could give him a ride to the train station in Roseville. He was getting anxious and wanted to get back to the Bay Area. Antsy and restless, just like me at the age of twenty-three, he'd already traveled to more than twenty different countries after graduating high school, with a backpack and a New Zealand passport. He'd even visited Iraq and Iran.

The next morning, we drove together to meet the train. As we looked out into the humongous train yard, I told him of the time, in the seventies, when bombs destined for Vietnam blew up there.

"I heard it all the way from Linda. That was a turbulent time."

"Like now?"

"Yes. Like now, but in a different way."

Amtrak's *California Corridor*, which operates from Auburn to San Jose, pulled in front of us and we got out of the van. I gave my son a hug and thanked him for his visit. I watched as he and other passengers boarded the train, most of them probably heading back to school or home after a Christmas holiday visit.

I gazed at the train as it slowly chugged away, thinking of the time when I left my hometown so many years ago. When I left Linda, and all the star thistles of Yuba County, far behind.

THE END

Afterword

Maree in front of cruise ship she couldn't board

We had decided to go "all out" for our fortieth wedding anniversary on July 1st and join other couples from our 1982 wedding group on a Caribbean cruise.

During embarkation, an official asked to see my passport. Looking at my New Zealand passport like it was some strange foreign object (which it kind of is) they then asked me if I had a visa.

Thank goodness! I had remembered to bring proof of my being a Permanent Legal Alien, and promptly whipped out my Green Card.

It took only seconds for the eagle-eyed Miami official to notice the expiration date.

"Excuse me ma'am, but you'll have to step aside and speak with a supervisor. This expired six months ago." I had no idea.

Denied boarding onto the cruise ship, I tried in vain to argue and plead my case. I also called Bob, who was already on the boat, and reported the bad news. I told him he could still go if he wanted to, and I could stay with a friend of a friend in Miami.

True to character, my faithful husband decided to abandon his cruise companions along with his dreams of visiting several Caribbean islands over a seven-day period.

We made the most of our disappointing situation and spent a memorable week with Mr. Richard Hayashi, our gracious Miami host, before returning to California.

That kind of symbolizes our marriage: we take the good with the bad and just hang in there, side by side.

In 1983, while we were still a newly wedded couple, my parents tried unsuccessfully to get me to abandon my faith and my marriage, both of which they opposed rather passionately.

I resisted and prevailed, much to the relief of my husband.

Without actually verbalizing it, I think we both felt more determined than ever to build an awesome marriage, if only to prove my parents wrong!

Four children and many years later, after much encouragement and prodding by Bob, I wrote a memoir about that "deprogramming" experience. Free Maree would never have happened without my husband's unflinching support. He even learned the nuts and bolts of self-publishing in order to magically birth my book into the world of Kindle and Amazon. (Which included printing my book in Australia and New Zealand. Plus building a sound booth and audio-engineering so I could create an audio book.)

It seemed only fair that I should reciprocate and be a true helpmate in Bob's own memoir writing journey. Fortunately, I really am the pavement to his dirt road, having studied Latin, French, art, classical piano, and English Literature.

Thanks to my various skills, I was able to support the long and stressful task of producing Leaving Linda as its Number One critic, copy editor, illustrator, and cheerleader.

I can testify that Bob, even if his spelling is not that great, is a true writer. He has sweated over Leaving Linda out in his little man cave for countless hours. He has an eye for good stories and is able to recount them with heart and humor, often self-deprecating.

And of course, this is no ordinary memoir. It is Bob's coming of age story in which he undergoes a religious conversion experience which radically changes his life's direction. In my opinion, he handles the sensitive topic of religion with skill and well-grounded common sense.

It is not easy to throw in your lot with new religious leaders such as Rev Moon and his wife, who even now, are subject to widespread misunderstanding, criticism, and persecution.

These days, our children and their generation are faced with the same dilemma we have confronted for over forty years: trust and have faith, or cave in to the world's view that this is just another manipulative cult?

Whatever you, the reader, decide, Bob and I are in it for the long haul.

Maree Gauper
September, 2022.

Acknowledgements

"To CAROL who willed this book" reads the dedication in John Steinbeck's depression-era historical novel, *The Grapes of Wrath*, the story of a destitute family departing Oklahoma to find work in California's Central Valley (in which Marysville, California is mentioned four times).

Carol was Steinbeck's first wife and as Dr. William Ray in *Steinbeck Now* writes, "She became his muse and motivator, typist and editor, connector and companion." In addition, the book's title was her idea.

I know I ain't no John Steinbeck, but I'm inspired to discover even he needed some help. Apart from typist, my wife Maree was all those things above, for me. She also conceived the *Leaving Linda* title as well as the *A Moonie from the Boonies* sub-title (so don't blame me, Unificationists). Plus, I'm especially grateful for her illustrations.

Without Maree's help, I doubt this memoir would have ever been written.

I would also like to thank my parents. My mother, for her willingness to challenge old beliefs and stereotypes, and my father for his World War II sacrifices and his examples of kindness toward others (even Republicans, with whom he seldom agreed).

Thank you, Susan McNally, for the Marysville Writers' Group and your constant pleas to "tell them how you feel!" And to fellow scribblers Roger and Diane Funston, Becky Davis, and Elise Boon, for your encouragement and input.

Thank you, dear beta-readers, for spending your precious time to read and critique my manuscript: Kimmy Brown, Paul Carlson, Chuck and Lesley Champlin, Stephen Child, Romilly Fraser, Sam Harley (notice how different the Introduction is per your suggestion), Bill Highland, Sue Kennedy, Jeff Scharfen, my sisters Karen Moore and Mary Sweet, and daughters In Mee and Una.

Special thanks to always-encouraging, forward-thinking Foreword writer Larry Moffitt.

Special, special thanks to Michael Kellett, aka Peter Saunders, for stopping me as I strolled along Seattle's waterfront the summer of 1978. Your invitation to attend the International Dinner changed my life.

Thank you, Reverend Moon, for picking me out of the dumpster.

Lastly, thank you God. For children, music, creation, creativity and your love and guidance.

About Author

Known as the Mark Twain of his former writers' group, Bob likes to weave tales of growin' up in the small Northern California town of Linda, and life as an often-maligned Unificationist, aka "Moonie". In 1982, in the Grand Ballroom of the New Yorker Hotel, which by the way is the same place where Hillary Clinton gave her failed presidential bid concession speech, he met his future copyeditor/illustrator wife, a New Zealander. Eventually they had several children, all of whom went to college and unlike their parents, have never been arrested for selling candy for their church.

A longtime Toastmaster, Bob has won several humorous speaking contests. In only one of them was he the only participant. Like John Lennon he dreams of a world of peace and no religion, especially schismatic ones that wear wacky bullet crowns. Additionally, he hopes for a world where yard sale people will promptly take down their signs and remove their listings from Facebook Marketplace after their sale is over. Plus learn the differences between sell and sale, and winch and wench.

To learn more about this amazing human being, and to get Bob's recipes for "The best fried catfish in St. Louis" and Korean pickled watermelon rind, or to download his "Deprogrammed!" board game, visit his "homemade and dated" website leavinglinda.com.